OUTPUT MEASURES and MORE

Planning and Evaluating Public Library Services for YOUNG ADULTS

Part of the Public Library Development Program

Virginia A. Walter

Young Adult Library Services Association

Public Library Association

American Library Association

Chicago and London 1995

Managing Editor: Joan Grygel

Index compiled by Carol Kelm

Cover design and composition by Charles Bozett in Garamond and Frutiger on a Macintosh IIcx using QuarkXPress 3.3

Printed on 50-pound Southshore Offset, a pH-neutral stock, and bound in 10 point C1S by IPC, St. Joseph, Michigan

The paper used in this publication meets the minimum requirements of American National Standard for Information Sciences--Permanence of Paper for Printed Library Materials, ANSI Z39.48-1992 ∞

Library of Congress Cataloging-in-Publication Data

Walter, Virginia A.
Output measures and more : planning and evaluating public library services for young adults / Virginia A. Walter.
p. cm.
"Part of the Public library development program."
Includes index.
ISBN 0-8389-3452-8
1. Public libraries—Services to teenagers—United States.
2. Public libraries—Services to teenagers—United States—Evaluation. I. Title.
Z718.5.W35 1995
027.62'6—dc20 95-15216

Printed in the United States of America.

99 98 97 96 95 5 4 3 2 1

Contents

Appendixes

Figures

Presidents' Message

The Young Adult Library Services Association (YALSA) and the Public Library Association (PLA) are committed to the improvement of library practice and library services. The leaders in both associations were delighted, therefore, when the opportunity came to cooperate on a venture that would develop particular techniques for planning and evaluating public library services for young adults, a segment of the population that accounts for as much as 23 percent of the total library usage, according to a recent federal government survey.

In the late 1980s, the Bureau of Library Programs in the Office of Educational Research and Improvement of the U.S. Department of Education funded the publication of *Output Measures for Public Library Service to Children: A Manual of Standardized Procedures* by Virginia A. Walter (Chicago: American Library Association, 1992). This companion volume to *Planning and Role Setting for Public Libraries: A Manual of Options and Procedures* by Charles R. McClure et al. (Chicago: American Library Association, 1987) and *Output Measures for Public Libraries,* second edition, by Nancy A. Van House et al. (Chicago: American Library Association, 1987) addressed the need to apply general measurement techniques to a more specialized aspect of library service. In the spring of 1993, Ray Fry, the director of Library Programs, approached YALSA and PLA and invited the divisions to submit a proposal to develop output measures for public library services to young adults. The proposal was submitted as a subcontract to "Evaluating Library Programs and Services," a project of the School of Library and Information Studies at the University of Wisconsin–Madison. This program, also funded through the U.S. Department of Education, Office of Educational Research and Improvement, Library Programs, was developed to train personnel in state library agencies to plan and conduct evaluations of library programs and services through institutes and through publications to support planning and evaluation. It was determined that the publication of a document about planning and evaluating young adult services in public libraries would be helpful in meeting the objectives of the Wisconsin project.

The proposal was developed quickly, approved by the YALSA and PLA boards of directors, and submitted by the School of Library and Information Studies. The U.S. Department of Education approved the funding, and Linda Waddle, deputy executive director of YALSA, was named the project director. Virginia Walter was hired as the principal investigator, and a joint PLA/YALSA advisory committee was formed.

As presidents of PLA and YALSA during the publication year of *Output Measures and More: Planning and Evaluating Public Library Services for Young Adults,* we are proud of the result of our collaborative work. We appreciate the hard work and thoughtful consideration that went into its preparation. We congratulate Virginia Walter for the fine job she has done in developing the concepts and techniques that are presented here, coordinating the field research, and writing the book. We also join Virginia in thanking the many people and institutions who participated in the effort. A special thanks to the faculty of the School of Library and Information Studies at the University of Wisconsin–Madison for their cooperation and to Ray Fry for his continuing support of youth services in public libraries.

We join with our members in PLA and YALSA in urging the widespread adoption of the management tools for planning and evaluating public library services for young adults that are presented in this book. We are confident that improved library services for young people and for entire communities will be the result.

Judith Drescher, President
Public Library Association, 1994–1995

Jennifer Jung Gallant, President
Young Adult Library Services Association, 1994–1995

Acknowledgments

Output Measures and More is a thoroughly collaborative effort. Sponsored by a partnership between the the School of Library and Information Studies of the University of Wisconsin–Madison, the Young Adult Library Services Association (YALSA), and the Public Library Association (PLA), it is a good example of what can happen when the library community decides to join together to accomplish a mutual goal.

The author gratefully acknowledges the assistance of the following people and organizations. This book truly could not have been written without their help.

- U.S. Department of Education, Library Research and Demonstration Program, with a special thanks to Ray Fry
- Jane Robbins, who provided support and leadership at the School of Library and Information Studies, University of Wisconsin–Madison
- Linda Waddle, Merri Monks, and the rest of the staff in the YALSA office at ALA Headquarters
- Project consultant Mary K. Chelton
- Project evaluator Douglas L. Zweizig
- Patrick Jones, who acted as unofficial consultant, offered his library as a test site, and gave consistent support and enthusiasm for the project
- Sean Dreilinger, whose eloquent photographs add a special dimension to the book, and to the staff and young adult patrons of the libraries at which he took pictures
- San Diego County Public Library: Linda Vista, Rancho Penasquitos, Logan Heights/Barrio Logan, East San Diego, and Tierrasanta Branches
- Ogden (Utah) High School
- Horace Mann Elementary School (Utah)

YALSA/PLA Advisory Committee for Young Adult Output Measures

- Elaine Meyers, Phoenix (Ariz.) Public Library
- Amy Oxley, Johnson County (Greenwood, Ind.) Public Library
- Kathleen Reif, Baltimore County (Md.) Public Library
- Jody Stefansson, Polytechnic School (Pasadena, Calif.)

Pretest Sites

- Long Beach (Calif.) Public Library
  - Antonia Herrera
  - Cordelia Howard
  - Nancy Messineo
- Santa Monica (Calif.) Public Library
  - Winifred Allard
  - Nancy Guidry
  - Ami Kirby
- Ventura County (Calif.) Library Services Agency
  - Dixie Adeniran
  - Julie Albright
  - Sunny Church

Field Test Sites

- Allen County (Fort Wayne, Ind.) Public Library
  - Stella Baker
  - Patrick Jones
- Boston (Mass.) Public Library
  - Catherine Clancy
- King County (Wash.) Library System
  - Susan Madden

Winter Park (Fla.) Public Library
Robert Melanson
Ann Cook
Carole Fiore (State Library of Florida)

Manuscript Readers

Carolyn Anthony, Skokie (Ill.) Public Library
Stella Baker, Allen County (Fort Wayne, Ind.) Public Library
Clara Bohrer, West Bloomfield Township (Mich.) Public Library
Audra Caplan, Baltimore County (Md.) Public Library
Mary K. Chelton, *Voice of Youth Advocates* (Metuchen, N.J.)
Sunny Church, Ventura County (Calif.) Library Services Agency
Catherine Clancy, Boston (Mass.) Public Library
Ann Cook, Winter Park (Fla.) Public Library
Judith Druse, Washburn University (Topeka, Kans.)
Marijo Duncan, Saguaro Branch Library (Phoenix, Ariz.)
Carole Fiore, State Library of Florida
Marilee Foglesong, New York Public Library
Jennifer Jung Gallant, Cleveland (Ohio) Public Library
June Garcia, San Antonio (Tex.) Public Library
Audrey Gorman, Library Power (Chicago, Ill.)
Nancy Guidry, Santa Monica (Calif.) Public Library
Antonia Herrera, Long Beach (Calif.) Public Library
Susan Horiuchi, Hawaii State Library
Patrick Jones, Tecumseh Branch Library (Fort Wayne, Ind.)
LaDonna Kienitz, City of Newport Beach (Calif.)
James Liesener, University of Maryland
Sarah Ann Long, North Suburban (Wheeling, Ill.) Library System
Mary Jo Lynch, ALA, Office for Research (Chicago, Ill.)
Susan Madden, King County (Wash.) Library System
Sylvia Mavrogenes, Miami-Dade (Fla.) Public Library System
Nancy Messineo, Long Beach (Calif.) Public Library
Elaine Meyers, Phoenix (Ariz.) Public Library
George Needham, ALA, Public Library Association (Chicago, Ill.)
Sandra Nelson, Tennessee State Library and Archives
Elizabeth O'Donnell, Manchester (N.H.) City Library
Amy Oxley, Johnson County (Greenwood, Ind.) Public Library
Art Plotnik, American Library Association (Chicago, Ill.)
Kathleen Reif, Baltimore County (Md.) Public Library
Mary Somerville, Miami-Dade (Fla.) Public Library System
Carol Starr, Benicia (Calif.) Public Library
Jody Stefansson, Polytechnic School (Pasadena, Calif.)
Deborah Taylor, Enoch Pratt Free Library (Baltimore, Md.)
Linda Waddle, American Library Association, Young Adult Services Association (Chicago, Ill.)
Ann Carlson Weeks, ALA, American Association of School Librarians and Young Adult Library Services Association (Chicago, Ill.)
Evie Wilson-Lingbloom, Mill Creek (Wash.) Library
Pat Woodrum, Tulsa (Okla.) City County Library System
Douglas Zweizig, University of Wisconsin–Madison

Research Assistance

Melissa Gross and Elizabeth Palmer, Graduate School of Library and Information Science, University of California, Los Angeles

Spanish Language Translation

Clemencia Aramburo, Graduate School of Library and Information Science, University of California, Los Angeles

Introduction

Output Measures and More: Planning and Evaluating Public Library Services for Young Adults is based on the more-general processes for planning and evaluation presented in two earlier Public Library Development Project (PLDP) documents, *Planning and Role Setting in Public Libraries* and *Output Measures for Public Libraries: A Manual of Standardized Procedures,* second edition. It is intended to help librarians and library administrators understand, rationalize, and improve their services to young adult customers. It will also be useful to library educators and students of library science.

Young adult specialists in public libraries are another obvious audience for this book. They have long wanted management tools to help them more rationally approach their work with young people and to evaluate and describe the results of their efforts in language that library administrators find valid. Unfortunately, young adult librarians have become a scarce commodity. A 1994 survey report by the National Center for Education Statistics (NCES) estimates that only 11 percent of the public libraries in the United States have a young adult specialist. According to the same report, however, 23 percent of the library patrons in 1994 were young adults between the ages of 12 and 18. These young adult patrons were served by young adult specialists or generalists in 45 percent of public libraries, by adult services librarians in 22 percent, by children's librarians in 12 percent, and by reference librarians in 5 percent. Interestingly enough, these figures do not differ significantly from an earlier 1988 survey.

All youth-serving librarians, whether they have the title of young adult librarian or not, should be interested in quantifying the work they do with this significant segment of their clientele. This book offers a broad menu of options for both planning and evaluating library services for young adults. It is designed to help librarians serving youth to meet many of the competencies recommended by the Young Adult Library Services Association (YALSA) in the document, *Young Adults Deserve the Best: Competencies for Librarians Serving Youth*.

The NCES findings about young adult usage should also arouse the interest of public library decision makers, including directors and trustees. If 23 percent of the library's customers are young adults, it makes sense for librarians to put some time and effort into understanding this significant user block and to ask questions such as: Have you

accounted for young adult usage in your planning? Are you considering young adults when you make your budget? Are you measuring this usage and reporting it to the policy-makers in your community? This manual will help you understand young adult usage of your library. The results should help to provide services to young adults more effectively and perhaps to integrate those services more seamlessly into the overall plan of library operations.

The political buzz words "youth at risk" may have become overused. Nevertheless, there are some compelling indicators that far too many adolescents in this country are at risk of not reaching their full potential as healthy, contributing adults in our society. Poverty, lack of educational and economic opportunities, adverse environmental conditions, and inadequate family supports contribute to this undesirable situation. We are beginning to understand that the task of reaching young adults and helping them to develop the skills, knowledge, and values necessary for becoming productive adults is not the job of isolated educational or social welfare institutions. Rather, it is the job of all institutions in a community, including the public library. Public libraries were mentioned specifically in *A Matter of Time: Risk and Opportunity in the Out-of-School Hours* (New York: Carnegie Corporation of New York, 1992), a report prepared by the Carnegie Council on Adolescent Development, as an important after-school resource for adolescents. As of this writing, library lobbyists in Washington, D.C., are working with legislators to include public libraries as agencies that could qualify for funding to provide crime prevention services and activities for young people. Around the country, local governmental and nonprofit initiatives are focusing on community partnerships that target youth at risk. Public libraries could and should participate in these coalitions. If they have done the kind of planning and evaluating of their current service levels to young adults that this book suggests, they will be in a much better position to do so. Many of the suggestions for conducting needs assessments and measuring outputs also could be used in grant preparation and administration.

There are few public libraries in the United States that have not felt some effect of recent efforts to "reinvent government." This term was popularized by David Osborne and Ted Gaebler, the authors of *Reinventing Government: How the Entrepreneurial Spirit Is Transforming the Public Sector* (Reading, Mass.: Addison-Wesley, 1992). Their model of a less-bureaucratic, more-responsive public sector has been adopted as a guide by federal agencies and by many local governments. This model emphasizes competition and enterprise as values to be incorporated into government. It is a customer-driven approach, with a strong emphasis on both mission and results. It requires government agencies to be accountable for returning value for taxpayers' investments in their programs. The planning and evaluation approach presented in this book is consistent with this new model of government.

The PLDP, a project of the Public Library Association of the American Library Association (ALA), anticipated this trend in government with the publication of *Output Measures for Public Libraries: A Manual of Standardized Procedures,* second edition, and *Planning and Role Setting for Public Libraries* in 1987. These two manuals gave public libraries a common language for talking about what they do and standardized techniques for measuring the results. *Output Measures for Public Library Service to Children: A Manual of Standardized Procedures* by Virginia Walter (Chicago: American Library Association, 1992) showed how the planning and measurement techniques could be adapted to one important market segment of public library users. The current book is a companion to the earlier three volumes. If you are already using general output measures, this manual will show you how to adapt them to services for young adults. If you have not started to use output measures in your library, this book may give you sufficient motivation to begin.

Definitions of Terms

Output is a term from the vocabulary of systems analysis. In the classic formulation of a system, *inputs* are those resources and raw materials that fuel the system. They are transformed within the system in a process sometimes called *throughput* and emerge as products or services called *outputs.* In a public library, *inputs* are resources such as personnel, books, and other library materials. These resources are given added value through such processes as training, cataloging, and strategic planning in the throughput segment of the library system. Customers interact with the system, and the results are the outputs: circulation, program attendance, answered questions, etc.

Output measures are ways to quantify the products of a system, or the quantitative measures of a system's outputs. Therefore, output measures for library service to young adults quantify a library's services and programs for young adults. They express the observable, empirical results of the library's services and programs for young adults in standardized, numerical terms.

What is a young adult? Adolescence is not a finite concept. Rather, it is a social construction, variously defined over time and in different circumstances. YALSA defines a young adult as someone between the ages of 12 and 18. The 1994 NCES survey asked public libraries to define young adults by age. The average definition was the same as the YALSA age definition. On the other hand, the Association for Library Service to Children (ALSC), also a division of ALA, defines children as anyone from birth through age 14. However, public libraries that responded to the NCES survey for children used an average definition of birth through age 12. In other words, for some purposes, people ages 12, 13, and 14 are children; at other times they are young adults. Christy Tyson, a former YALSA president, observed that many libraries organize young adult services based on the local configuration of schools.

Therefore, when you begin to implement output measures that are segmented by age, be clear about how *you* are defining a young adult. If you are using the definitions set forth in *Output Measures for Public Library Service to Children,* young adults will probably be defined as library users who are ages 15 through 18. If you follow the YALSA definition, services to young adults begin at age 12. In any case, do not overlap in the measurement efforts. Avoid counting the same library user as both a child and a young adult. Establish clear age definitions for purposes of data collection and stick to them.

Overview of the Measures

Throughout the book, particular output measures are identified by the use of bold type: **Young Adult Information Transactions per Young Adult.** Data elements, the building blocks of each measure, are printed in all capital letters: YOUNG ADULT POPULATION OF SERVICE AREA and ANNUAL NUMBER OF YOUNG ADULT INFORMATION TRANSACTIONS.

The output measures in this book are organized in seven basic categories: library use, materials use, materials availability, information services, programming, community relations, and youth participation. They are summarized here, but for a more detailed discussion of each one, see Part 3.

Library Use

- **Young Adult Library Visits per Young Adult** is the number of visits to the library by young adults per young adult in the community served. It measures walk-in use of the library.
- **Building Use by Young Adults** indicates the average number of young adults who are in the library at any one time. This measure indicates patterns of use.
- **Furniture/Equipment Use by Young Adults** reports the proportion of time, on average, that a particular type of furniture or piece of equipment, such as computer terminals or lounge seating, is in use by young adults.
- **Homework Center Visits per Young Adult** is the number of young adults using the homework center relative to the number of young adults in the community served.

Materials Use

- **Circulation of Young Adult Materials per Young Adult** measures the annual use of young adult materials loaned for use outside the library relative to the number of young adults in the community served.
- **Circulation of Materials per Young Adult** measures the annual use of all library materials loaned for use outside the library to young adults relative to the number of young adults in the community served.
- **In-Library Use of Young Adult Materials per Young Adult** indicates the annual use of young adult materials within the library relative to the number of young adults in the community served.
- **In-Library Use of Materials by Young Adults per Young Adult** measures the annual use of materials from all parts of the collection by young adults within the library relative to the number of young adults in the community served.
- **Turnover Rate of Young Adult Materials** measures the annual circulation of young adult materials relative to the total size of the young adult collection. It indicates the average circulation of each item in the young adult collection.

Materials Availability

- **Young Adult Fill Rate** is the percentage of searches for library materials by young adults that are successful.
- **Young Adult Homework Fill Rate** is the percentage of searches for library materials for homework use by young adult library users that are successful.

Information Services

- **Young Adult Information Transactions per Young Adult** is the annual number of information transactions (reference or readers' advisory queries) by young adult library users per young adult in the community served.
- **Young Adult Information Transaction Completion Rate** is the percentage of information transactions by young adult library users that are completed successfully.

Programming

- **Young Adult Program Attendance per Young Adult** measures annual attendance at young adult library programs relative to the number of young adults in the community served.
- **Program Attendance per Young Adult** measures annual attendance at all library programs by young adults relative to the number of young adults in the community served.

Community Relations

- **Young Adult School Contact Rate** is the annual number of contacts with schools serving young adults made by library staff relative to the total number of schools serving young adults.
- **Annual Number of Young Adult Community Contacts** is the total number of contacts in a given year made by library staff with community organizations, institutions, or individuals (excluding schools) on behalf of public library service to young adults.

Youth Participation

- **Young Adult Participation Rate** is the number of young adults who participate in voluntary service activities at the library relative to the number of young adults in the community.
- **Annual Number of Young Adult Volunteer Hours** is the total number of hours worked by young adult volunteers in the library during a given year.

How This Book Is Organized

Part 1 revisits the planning and role setting process formulated by the Public Library Association (PLA) and shows how to apply this process to library service to young adults. It demonstrates how to conduct a community-based needs assessment targeted at young adults. This section also includes directions for developing vision and mission statements and choosing and/or implementing public library roles for a young adult population. Information is included about preparing goals and objectives and building a service plan that meets the needs identified in the planning process.

Part 2 looks more closely at how to evaluate the results of library services and programs for young adults. It provides tips for managing the measurement process in a particular library situation. General guidelines are given for collecting and analyzing data, as well as for interpreting and acting on the results. This section also includes information about two qualitative data-gathering techniques—interviews and focus groups—that can be used to enrich quantitative measures.

Finally, Part 3 covers the output measures themselves. A capsule summary of each measure gives the definition, the formula for calculation, the method for data collection, and an example. This summary is followed by detailed instructions for collecting the data for that measure, calculating the result, interpreting it, and following up with appropriate actions. In some cases there are suggestions for further modifications or variations of the measure.

The final section is an appendix of ready-to-photocopy forms for all the measures. Forms

intended for use with the general public also have Spanish-language translations. In most cases, the forms may be used straight from the book with no modification. If necessary, however, they can be adapted to specific local needs.

Using This Manual

If you are familiar with the PLDP planning and role setting process and the use of output measures, you will soon feel comfortable with this book. It uses the same format, vocabulary, and approach as the three earlier books in the PLDP series, *Planning and Role Setting for Public Libraries; Output Measures for Public Libraries: A Manual of Standardized Procedures,* second edition; and *Output Measures for Public Library Service to Children.* However, the particular nature of library service to young adults dictates some new and different measures and data-collection techniques that differ from those in the earlier manuals.

If you are new to planning and role setting or evaluating library services with output measures, begin by reading Parts 1 and 2 for an overview. After deciding which measures to implement, look more carefully at those specific measures in Part 3.

Read through the directions for each measure carefully and try to imagine how you are going to implement them, one step at a time, in your own library. Taking the time to outline in your mind exactly how you will do each step in your library will make the directions more concrete and meaningful. When you actually have the data in hand, you will find that the mathematical calculations of the actual measures are easy. All you need is a calculator and the ability to follow directions.

Sources for Additional Information

A Matter of Time: Risk and Opportunity in the Out-of-School Hours. New York: Carnegie Council on Adolescent Development, Carnegie Corporation of New York, 1992.

A report that shows how families, schools, and community organizations need to change to meet the changing needs of young adolescents.

McClure, Charles R., et al. *Planning and Role Setting for Public Libraries.* Chicago: American Library Association, 1987.

A basic guide to planning for public libraries.

Osborne, David, and Ted Gaebler. *Reinventing Government: How the Entrepreneurial Spirit Is Transforming the Public Sector.* Reading, Mass.: Addison-Wesley, 1992.

The influential book that outlines the characteristics of a more entrepreneurial, responsive public sector.

Survey on Library Services for Young Adults in Public Libraries. Washington, D.C.: U.S. Department of Education, Office of Educational Research and Improvement, National Center for Education Statistics, 1994.

A Fast Response Survey Report that gives a statistical overview of public library service to young adults as reported by the public libraries.

Tyson, Christy. "What's in a Name?" *School Library Journal* 36 (Dec. 1990): 47.

A discussion of the difficulties of defining the population served by young adult library specialists.

Van House, Nancy A., et al. *Output Measures for Public Libraries: A Manual of Standardized Procedures,* 2d ed. Chicago: American Library Association, 1987.

Basic measurement techniques for quantifying the outcomes of public library service.

Walter, Virginia A. *Output Measures for Public Library Service to Children: A Manual of Standardized Procedures.* Chicago: American Library Association, 1992.

Measurement techniques for quantifying and analyzing the outcomes of public library service to children.

Young Adults Deserve the Best: Competencies for Librarians Serving Youth. Chicago: Young Adult Services Division/American Library Association, n.d.

A systematic listing of the competencies required of librarians who provide public library services for young adults.

Applying the Planning and Role Setting Process to Library Services for Young Adults

PART 1

Although *Planning and Role Setting for Public Libraries* (PRSPL) does not address the need to plan for young adults who use the public library, it is a detailed manual that provides an overview of the planning process. When libraries plan for young adults, certain aspects of the planning process may need more attention than they receive in PRSPL.

It is particularly important to involve young adults in the planning process. Many libraries have young adult advisory groups, and they should be involved in decision-making processes in the library. If such a group does not exist, this would be the time to start one. Young adults can assist with all phases of the planning process.

A needs assessment will help you identify the young adults in your community. It will also help you understand what their lives are like, what other organizations and agencies provide services for them, and what they expect and need from the library.

When you have a good understanding of the young adults in the community, a plan to serve them can be formulated. Library roles may be selected that pertain to service to young adults only.

Library mission and vision statements may be written for "all ages," but statements can also be written that are specific to the library's service to young adults. Goals and objectives flow directly from vision and mission statements and can be also written for service to young adults.

The PLA Planning and Role Setting Process

The authors of *Planning and Role Setting for Public Libraries* (PRSPL) describe a planning process that is dynamic and flexible, designed to help public libraries of all sizes achieve visions of excellence that are specific to local communities. Based on earlier work by Ernest de Prospo, this process involves gathering information about the library and its community, selecting roles and defining a vision, setting goals and objectives, developing activities that will help the library reach those goals and objectives, reporting the results of the planning efforts, and evaluating what is going on. The planning process is seen as a necessary management function, enabling the library to make the best fit between what the community wants and needs and what the library can provide.

PRSPL is a detailed manual for implementing a planning process in public libraries, providing many options for levels of effort. Many helpful workforms are provided, which can be photocopied and used "as is" or adapted to particular cases. No reliable data are currently available on the number or percentage of public libraries that have adapted this planning and role setting process, but the vocabulary and concepts have become widely known in the public library community since the publication of the manual in 1987.

The Public Library Association is currently evaluating PRSPL and its companions, *Output Measures for Public Libraries,* second edition, and *Output Measures for Public Library Service to Children.* It is likely that some changes will be made in emphasis and approach. Certainly the increased use of electronic information technology and the concept of a "library without walls" will be incorporated in the next edition. In the meantime, the 1987 publication provides a good basic approach to planning that all public libraries can adopt and adapt.

PRSPL does not identify young adults as a particular segment of the community to be targeted or analyzed. However, a good general strategic plan for any public library will identify young adults as one significant segment of users. It is also possible that a library might want to develop a plan of service specifically for young adults. This section will be helpful in either case.

Organizational Considerations

As noted in the introduction, only 11 percent of all public libraries in the United States have specialized young adult librarians. Nevertheless, young adults are active consumers of public library services, making up an average of 23 percent of the

total library user population. How libraries plan to deliver effective service to this segment of the population will depend on a number of political and organizational considerations.

Some libraries do not organize their services by age distinctions; rather, generalists serve all segments of the population. However, these libraries will benefit from a systematic needs assessment of their young adult user base to guide the generalists in their efforts to provide appropriate collections, services, and programs. Ordinarily this assessment would be done as part of the regular planning process of the library. To make sure that young adults are not overlooked, the director or staff person responsible for overseeing the planning effort should assign someone the specific responsibility of conducting the young adult user needs assessment and incorporating the findings into the overall plan.

Another common pattern is the assignment of responsibility for service to young adults to either an adult reference librarian or to the children's librarian. The individual designated as the young adult librarian, whether he or she has the actual title or not, should be an active participant in the planning process and should be charged with representing the interests of young adults.

Making a special effort to look at young adults as a unique and special segment of the user population during the planning process should result in an awareness of how the library's overall mission and roles affect service to young people. The goal is to make young people visible to library decision makers and to help librarians consider the particular needs of young adults when they develop their service plans. The result may be a separate planning document or a section of the overall plan that is devoted to library service to young adults or a seamless integration of youth services into the entire plan.

Library directors or those who have the authority to make the decision to develop a young adult service plan may skip the next section. Librarians who are lower in the hierarchy, however, may need to convince higher administrators of the benefits of devoting some effort to planning specifically for library service to young adults. Following are some possible selling points.

1. Cite the NCES survey that indicates young adults make up 23 percent of the library users nationally. How does your library compare? Wouldn't it be a good idea to find out?
2. Any market segment that accounts for 23 percent of your usage is too important to be taken for granted. It makes good sense to develop the young adult market as a natural niche for public libraries. It also makes good marketing sense to be sure that you are building good customer loyalty so you don't lose your young adult patrons when they become adults. Consider how McDonald's has made marketing history with this strategy of building life-long users.
3. In many communities, young adults are the subject of much political rhetoric. Whether "youth at risk" or "education for the year 2000" strikes a chord in your community, there is a good chance that local politicians will come around at some point asking what the library is doing for teenagers. It would be a good idea to have statistics ready to show what the library is doing now and to indicate directions for future growth.
4. Many of the planning suggestions and measurement techniques in this manual are as useful for proposal and grant writing as they are for regular planning and evaluation. Evidence of systematic needs assessment is often required for successful grant applications. If the library does not conduct a formal planning process or the director is not eager to spend time integrating service to young adults into the planning process that you already have, direct your planning and measurement activities to grant applications instead.

Conducting the Needs Assessment

PRSPL calls the needs assessment part of the planning process "looking around." In this step, you gather information about the young adults in your community that will help you to decide which services would be most appropriate for your library to offer them.

Involve Young Adults in the Process

Whether you are contributing to a general library plan or creating a plan specifically for library service to young adults, teenagers can be effective participants in the process. As part of the planning team, they can help gather data, participate in focus groups, provide input for the selection of roles, and offer advice on aspects of a service plan. If you already have a young adult advisory council, the members can provide the leadership cadre for your planning team. If the library has

not yet formed such a youth advisory group, the prospect of an imminent young adult services planning project might be a good impetus to start one.

Be sure, however, that when you are collecting data from and about young adults in the community you also look outside the population of library users. Plan to get data from young adults who are not now active library users as well as from your regular library patrons. One good way to do this is to work with other existing organized groups of young adults. Ask the youth-group leader from a local religious organization or a gang counselor or a soccer coach if you could conduct a focus group with some of the young people with whom they work. Ask your contacts at the local schools to help you organize focus groups or interviews with students. Some of these young adults in the focus groups may be interested in becoming more involved with the library planning effort and help you reach out to parts of the community that you otherwise might have difficulty contacting.

Plan Your Approach

You must make some initial decisions. What information do you need to gather? How much effort can you put into this process? Who is available to do it? How are you going to use volunteers? One good way to start making these decisions is to look at Form 1, Young Adult Community Information Data Sheet. You will find it in Appendix B at the back of the book. Adapted from Workform C in PRSPL, this form will help you get a sense of the kind of information you might want to acquire. Check the data elements that seem most important to you and then try to assess how much effort it would take to collect the information.

Set a time line and assign responsibility to appropriate people for gathering the information. In the fine guidebook by Stan Weisner, *Information Is Empowering: Developing Library Services for Youth at Risk* (Oakland, Calif.: Bay Area Library and Information System, 1992), California librarians involved with the Bay Area Youth at Risk program advise that a reasonable time period for a thorough initial needs assessment is three to six months. After this first investment of time, maintaining and updating the information is less intensive.

Gather the Information

After you have decided what information would be most useful in helping you analyze the community, draw up your own young adult community information form, based on Form 1, parts A and B. This form will be your guide to the first two segments of data collection: demographics and organizations. For each element, determine how or where you are going to gather the information. Some good sources for statistical demographic data include census data and other government statistics, such as

Bureau of Labor statistics
school district records
local newspaper articles
local planning departments
Source Book of Demographic Data for Every Zip Code in the U.S.

After collecting basic statistical data, you will need to identify relevant organizations, institutions, agencies, and businesses. What organizations are serving the needs and interests of young adults? Form 2, Young Adult Community Organization Checklist, is a listing of many of these. You will probably think of others. Decide which of these are important to your community and gather information about them. Form 3, Young Adult Community Organization Data Sheet, indicates the kind of information that you might want to have for each relevant community organization. If you decide to make the effort to collect this information aggressively and thoroughly, you will have the nucleus of a good community information and referral file as well as valuable information to feed into the planning process. You will also have made some valuable community contacts.

For information on organizations and institutions, you can check such obvious sources as the yellow pages. In addition, see if a local agency or group has produced a directory of service providers. Find out what information is available from local elected officials and the Chamber of Commerce. Check with schools and the local United Way to see what resources they can share.

After checking all the printed sources you can find, you may want to use some other techniques from social science research methods. Ask "key informants"—knowledgeable young adults or young-adult service providers—to identify youth-serving agencies, organizations, or institutions. Also, ask young adult volunteers to draw up a list of businesses that are important to young people in the community.

Now that you have learned about the young adult demographics and youth-oriented organizations in your area, you are ready for the final aspect of data collection. This activity is a little more subjective. Try to get a sense of the life styles of young adults in the community. What is it like to be a teenager there? Are most young people in school? Do they plan to go to college when they finish? Do they have after-school or weekend jobs? What do they do in their free time? Where do they congregate? Are sports important? What radio stations are their favorites? Be aware that young adults tend to define themselves and their place in the adolescent community by their music. Unless yours is an unusually homogeneous community, there will probably be several segments, each defined by their music preferences. What television programs do they watch? What languages do they speak at home? How do they get from place to place? What are the big problems for young adults here? What do they like about the community? What worries them? Do they remain in the community as adults, or do they leave for other opportunities?

Interviews and focus groups with well-placed, sensitive adults or with the young adults themselves will help you find answers to these kinds of questions. Some examples of adult key informants who might be able to give you good insights are teachers; school library media specialists; gang counselors; public health and school nurses; coaches; recreation center staff; police officers; employees of music, video, sporting goods, and popular clothing stores; parents; and people just out of their teens who still live in the community.

You will also want to get a sense of what young adults say they want or need from the library. You can survey young adult library users to find out why they come to the library, what services they use, and what they would like to see added or improved. You also should try to get opinions from young adults who don't currently use the library. Focus groups or interviews are good techniques to use.

Sometimes young adults have well-articulated reasons for not using the library: "It's too far from my house." "I don't have transportation." "I'm too busy." "It's in Crips territory; I'm down with the Bloods." "My school library has everything I need." Often, however, it is just not something they think about. It is difficult for them to imagine what library services or resources might be useful to them. You need to give them something concrete to think about. One device used by a consultant in developing a strategic plan for a library in a nonprofit youth facility in an economically depressed area was to show the young adults in the focus groups blueprints of the proposed library. "Then," she asked, "what should we put in here?" The young adults had lots of good ideas.

If the community is multicultural or multiracial, be sure that you have looked around in all parts of the community. Use key informants to help you gather information in communities that might otherwise be less accessible to you.

Analyze the Information

Translating the information into an effective library response is not an easy task. Begin by organizing your data. You will have demographic statistics, lists of organizations and businesses, and narrative reports from focus groups. Individually, or as a planning group, look for surprises, patterns, and trends. Relate what you have learned about young adults in the community to information about the community as a whole. Try to see the information from different points of view, and try to link it to information needs. See if you can group data into four or five major findings.

For example, the statistical data may show that a surprisingly large percentage of the young adult population has dropped out of school. You are aware from the general community analysis that the light industry that was the major source of jobs has been moving out of the area. You have heard from young adults in focus groups that finding work is a major concern. Taken together, this information might point to one finding: Young adults need GED information and basic entry-level job skills.

Form 4, Looking Around Summary Sheet, taken from PRSPL, shows how to relate the major findings to library responses. Figure 1 takes the previously discussed example and shows how it might be interpreted on the form.

Developing a Plan for Library Service to Young Adults

Now that you have a good understanding of the young adults in the community, it is time to develop the plan itself. It will have six parts: library roles, mission statement, vision statement, goals and objectives, action steps, and evaluation strategies. Each of these sections will be discussed in turn.

Before beginning, however, you need to make additional important decisions about the process. Who will be selecting the roles and developing the mission and vision statement? Whose input will be solicited? If this is going to be a democratic, participatory process, you will need a mechanism for making group decisions. PRSPL has a good discussion of different approaches based on the levels of effort required for each.

Library Roles

PRSPL presents a menu of eight roles from which libraries can select those that best match the identified community needs and the resources of the particular library. The intent is for public libraries to focus their resources on doing a few things well rather than trying to be all things to all people. PRSPL recommends that small and medium-sized libraries select one primary role and two or three secondary roles on which to concentrate their efforts.

Libraries may select roles for the library as a whole or they may decide to select one set of roles for the central library and another set for branches. If a plan for service to young adults is being developed independently of an overall plan, the roles may pertain to library service to young adults only. If so, the roles still must relate to the overall library mission.

It is important to keep the library's resources, current activities, and the findings from the needs assessment in mind as the roles are selected. Form 5, Selecting Library Roles Work Sheet, is taken from PRSPL. It is a way of quantifying perceptions about current activities and desired levels of commitment for each role. If a group of people is participating in the process, you can tabulate everyone's scores and discuss the results. Some points to consider include:

Are there some roles in which current level and desired levels of commitment are similar?

Do different segments of the community want different desired levels of service?

Does everyone agree on current levels of service? If not, why not?

Does the library have the resources to take on the roles that have the highest ratings for the desired level of commitment?

Are there political considerations that might affect the selection of particular roles?

As the advocate for young adults throughout this process, you must try to ensure that their needs and interests are considered and included in final decisions. (In some cases, of course, there will be young adult participation in the process

Major Finding	Impact on Library Roles and Services	Opportunities	Possible Library Responses
1. High drop-out & unemployment rates—YAs = need job info, job skills	Independent Learning Center?	Partnership with Job Corps?	Add more GED books. Programming on job search strategies
2.			
3.			
4.			

Figure 1. Worked Example of Form 4: Looking Around Summary Sheet

itself.) Assume, for example, that Popular Materials Library is selected as the primary role. It is possible, of course, that this is the most important role for young adults as well as other age segments. However, if you know from your needs assessment that another role, such as Formal Education Support Services, is the most critical role for teenagers in the community, then you will lobby for that one to be adopted as a secondary role, if not the primary role.

None of the eight roles listed in Form 5 specifically targets young adults, but all of them can be applied to library service to young adults. In the following section, each role is introduced with the definition given in PRSPL. This introduction is followed by a discussion of how that role might be applied to young adults; it concludes with some output measures from this manual that you might want to consider if you were trying to implement that role.

1. *Community Activities Services:* "The library is a central focus point for community activities, meetings, and services."

   This role can be particularly significant in communities where public meeting space is a scarcity. It has been particularly effective in lower-income neighborhoods where community services are plentiful but fragmented and uncoordinated. The public library has sometimes been able to provide a central location for information and resource sharing by making its facility available to a wide range of community agencies.

   Library staff implementing this role are actively involved with other youth-serving individuals, agencies, and organizations. They take a leadership role in coordinating youth services in the community, functioning as both an information broker and an intermediary between other organizations.

   Groups of all kinds are encouraged to meet at the library. The library reaches out to youth organizations such as 4H, Scouts, and Explorers, as well as to those adult organizations that serve youth. Library staff may sponsor an organization for young people themselves.

   Programming is an important aspect of the service plan. The library offers the mix of educational, social, cultural, recreational, and informational programs that the community analysis indicated that young people needed. Youth participants may help plan and implement these programs for all ages.

   Cable television is an excellent medium for implementing this role. Young adults may be involved in the actual programming in addition to being the intended audience.

   A critical resource for this role is a staff that is committed to community outreach and competent in forming partnerships with external agencies. Meeting space also is an important factor. The materials collection is less important to this role than the staff and the physical facility.

   Output Measures to consider:

   Young Adult Library Visits per Young Adult
   Building Use by Young Adults
   Young Adult Program Attendance per Young Adult
   Program Attendance per Young Adult
   Annual Number of Young Adult Community Contacts
   Young Adult Participation Rate
   Annual Number of Young Adult Volunteer Hours

2. *Community Information Services:* "The library is a clearinghouse for current information on community organizations, issues, and services."

   Like the first role, this role requires that library staff be involved in the organized life of the community. The library acquires, organizes, and provides access to a broad range of community information that is relevant to young adults themselves, as well as to their parents and other youth service providers. This information could be about services such as job training or drug counseling, recreational opportunities, and cultural events or about local issues such as graffiti, gang violence, or curfews.

   Library staff provides community information in all appropriate formats—through bulletin boards, electronic databases, books, pamphlets, magazines, videotapes, audiocassettes, cable television programming, information and referral files, individual tutoring or counseling, and programs. The library may be an active participant in community electronic networks such as the Freenet. Young adults can be very helpful in identifying the information needs that should be addressed, maintaining bulletin boards, compiling referral files or databases of local information, locating nontraditional sources of information, and publicizing the library's resources. This information tends to become outdated very quickly, so special efforts must be made to keep files current.

   One critical resource for this role is a community-oriented staff that is skilled in acquiring, organizing, and disseminating time-dated, local information. Technical expertise in exploiting electronic information technologies and physical space for one-on-one tutoring or large programs are also desirable. Community analysis procedures should be ongoing.

Output Measures to consider:

Young Adult Library Visits per Young Adult
Building Use by Young Adults
Young Adult Program Attendance per Young Adult
Program Attendance per Young Adult
Annual Number of Young Adult Community Contacts
Young Adult Participation Rate
Annual Number of Young Adult Volunteer Hours

3. *Formal Education Support Services:* "The library assists students of all ages in meeting educational objectives established during their formal courses of study."

   Since most young adults are enrolled in a formal course of study, this role can be critical for libraries that emphasize youth services. The public library that selects this role works closely with teachers and school library media specialists in local schools and with the growing number of home school organizations to provide the services that are most needed by young adults.

   The collection is important to the successful implementation of this role. Libraries stock multiple copies of materials of frequently assigned book report titles. They may purchase materials that young adults use to complete homework assignments and supply electronic information sources such as multimedia encyclopedias and CD-ROM databases.

   In addition to providing materials that support the curriculum, libraries may want to offer additional services such as homework or tutoring centers staffed by paid or volunteer aides. Young adults may serve as peer tutors, helping other students to learn. Materials for hot topics that are currently in demand may be put on reserve. Textbooks may be available. Librarians may prepare bibliographies to guide students as they retrieve information needed for particular kinds of assignments.

   One critical resource for this role is a staff that is familiar with the curriculum, able to work with local educators, and skilled in helping young adults formulate and complete the information searches that are required for their homework assignments. The librarians are able to provide both formal and informal bibliographic instruction. In addition, the collection supports the curriculum needs of young adults, including the nontraditional provisions of some home schooling courses of study. It may be necessary, for example, to provide informational books with a fundamentalist Christian approach in some communities. Physical facilities may include a homework center and space for individual tutoring.

   Output Measures to consider:

   Young Adult Library Visits per Young Adult
   Building Use by Young Adults
   Furniture/Equipment Use by Young Adults (pinpointing those items of furniture or equipment that support formal education needs, such as the electronic Magazine Index, tutoring tables, etc.)
   Homework Center Visits per Young Adult
   In-Library Use of Materials by Young Adults per Young Adult
   Young Adult Homework Fill Rate
   Young Adult Information Transactions per Young Adult
   Young Adult Information Transaction Completion Rate
   Young Adult School Contact Rate
   Young Adult Participation Rate

4. *Independent Learning Center:* "The library supports individuals of all ages pursuing a sustained program of learning independent of any educational provider."

   The library provides materials and services to help young adults acquire skills and knowledge outside the formal curriculum. Many young adults have passionate avocations, ranging from computer programming to music to athletics to photography. A library positioned as an independent learning center can support those interests.

   Many of the skills that young people need to acquire on the way to adulthood are not addressed in school. Some libraries have found that programming that features such topics as "buying your first car," "finding a summer job," "babysitting basics," or "writing the college application essay" have helped to fill the gap. For young adults who have dropped out of school, the public library may be their only educational resource.

   Libraries trying to implement this role for young adults may find that these patrons need more guidance than do adults. Library staff must

be ready to assist teenagers as they formulate their independent learning strategies. The assistance and information may take many forms: traditional print materials, electronic resources, programming, workshops, and tutorials.

All of a library's resources can be called on for this role: staff, collection, and the physical facility itself. It is critical that all elements be focused on meeting the independent learning needs of individual young adults.

Output Measures to consider:

Young Adult Library Visits per Young Adult
Furniture/Equipment Use by Young Adults
In-Library Use of Materials by Young Adults per Young Adult
Young Adult Fill Rate
Program Attendance per Young Adult
Young Adult Program Attendance per Young Adult

5. *Popular Materials Library:* "The library features current, high-demand, high-interest materials in a variety of formats for persons of all ages."

Many public libraries have a young adult section that features popular young adult materials such as R. L. Stine and Christopher Pike paperbacks. If popular materials library is a highlighted role for the library, the young adult collection must be expanded and given some prominence. Bookstore-style shelving can highlight multiple copies of popular materials by allowing them to be displayed with the covers out. With this role in mind, library staff can be alert to new trends in young adult reading in their communities and respond quickly. They will know whether young adults using their library prefer to read books by Terry McMillan, Stephen King, or V. C. Andrews. In addition to popular books, popular magazines, cassette tapes, compact discs, and videos will be attractively displayed and available.

Young adults can help library staff to identify popular materials by serving as book reviewers and selection assistants. They can compile "top ten" lists of popular music groups to help librarians make selections. Librarians can make the peer reviews and lists available to other young adults and use them as guides in material selection.

Staff are knowledgeable about the collection and able to market it through both formal and impromptu book talks, the preparation of promotional book lists, and sensitive readers' advisory services.

The critical resources for this role are the materials collection as well as a staff that is sensitive to young adult interests and skilled in acquiring and marketing popular materials for young people. A physical facility with shelving and furniture that facilitates browsing also is desirable.

Output Measures to consider:

Circulation of Young Adult Materials per Young Adult
Circulation of Materials per Young Adult
Turnover Rate of Young Adult Materials
Young Adult Fill Rate

6. *Preschoolers' Door to Learning:* "The library encourages young children to develop an interest in reading and learning through services for children, and for parents and children together."

It might appear that this role specifically excludes young adults. However, some young adults are themselves parents of preschoolers. Others work with preschoolers as babysitters, after-school day care aides, or church school assistants. They may also serve as volunteer story readers to preschoolers in the library.

Specific library services for young adults might include outreach to schools and clinics serving pregnant teenagers, special sessions on children's literature in local high schools, or babysitting training programs. The library also may provide training in picture book read-aloud and flannel board or puppet techniques for young adult volunteer story hour assistants.

Critical resources for this role include a rich preschool collection featuring picture books, software, and realia appropriate for young children. The staff should be skilled in working with parents and care givers of all ages (including adolescents), as well as with preschool children. The physical facility should be inviting and safe for young children and families.

Output Measures to consider:

Circulation of Materials per Young Adult
In-Library Use of Materials by Young Adults per Young Adult
Young Adult Fill Rate
Program Attendance per Young Adult

Note that all of these measures could be segmented to look at the use of preschool and/or parenting materials by young adults or a particular kind of programming, such as preschool storytimes and/or parenting classes.

7. *Reference Center:* "The library actively provides timely, accurate, and useful information for community residents."

When this role is selected, care must be taken to ensure that young adults have access to all materials in all formats. Fees for some information services that discriminate against young adult patrons must be discouraged.

The library also will want to examine the quality of interactions between reference staff and young adults. Are young adults' questions treated with the same respect as adults' inquiries? Does the reference staff make an effort to make the young adult feel comfortable? Is the reference staff trained in the use of information tools that are specific to young adult interests? Does the reference staff refuse to answer some kinds of questions because they consider them to be trivial or improper? Are homework questions treated in the same way as any other question, or are young adults told to "look it up themselves"?

The collection should be evaluated to ensure that it supports the reference questions of young adults as well as those of adult patrons. The community analysis should help to identify the basic information needs likely to be addressed. Periodic focus groups with young adults can be useful. A young adult advisory council can provide ongoing guidance.

The critical resources for this role are the reference staff and the collection. Young adults are likely to draw from the entire collection in their reference needs, not just from the young adult collection. Cross-training may be necessary to ensure that all public service staff members are able to assist young adults using all areas of the collection.

Output Measures to consider:

In-Library Use of Materials by Young Adults per Young Adult
Young Adult Information Transactions per Young Adult
Young Adult Information Transaction Completion Rate

8. *Research Center:* "The library assists scholars and researchers to conduct in-depth studies, investigate specific areas of knowledge, and create new knowledge."

The important thing to remember about implementing this role for young adults is that young adults do sometimes conduct in-depth studies, investigate specific areas of knowledge, and create new knowledge. Whether it is work for a science fair or the advancement of a personal hobby, adolescents frequently do advanced research. Libraries that have adopted this role must be willing to treat young adults as serious scholars and researchers. Because many young adults may have been discouraged in other efforts to use specialized resources, libraries also may need to market their research services to them. Young adults doing family histories, for example, may not realize the resources that are available in a good genealogy collection.

Ordinarily a library will not select this role unless it has some special collections that it wishes to highlight. Another resource that is important for the implementation of this role for young adults is a library staff that is skilled in facilitating the information search process for teenagers and guiding them in the use of those collections.

Output Measures to consider:

Young Adult Information Transaction Completion Rate
In-Library Use of Materials by Young Adults per Young Adult
Furniture/Equipment Use by Young Adults (targeting special facilities such as a rare book room or genealogy collection)

Mission Statement

Roles are more useful to the library's internal decision makers than to the general public. Roles help the library to define its priorities and represent a kind of shared language for the people responsible for carrying out the library's mission.

The mission statement, on the other hand, is a statement of the library's purpose, its reason for existence. It is usually quite general. It may or may not mention the roles that have been selected, but it should be an umbrella under which those roles can comfortably be accommodated. It should communicate to the general public in nontechnical terms the library's business. The mission statement will probably not mention any particular segment of the community, such as young adults, but will instead use language like "all ages."

For example, a well-financed library in a suburban community has selected the primary role of reference services, with the secondary roles of popular materials library, formal education support services, and preschoolers' door to learning. Its mission statement reads:

> The Utopia Public Library is in the business of providing all people of this town with free access to all of the information they need to lead happy, productive, useful lives. The information is provided through a collection of materials in all formats, expert professional information services, and age-appropriate programs of all kinds.

You may want to develop an additional mission statement that is specific to the library's service to young adults. This statement should not conflict with the library's overall mission and may, in fact, be a parallel document that substitutes the phrase "young adults" for the more-general language. Developing a specialized mission statement serves the purpose of raising awareness of the library's responsibility to young adults. See what happens when just two words are changed in the Utopia Public Library's mission statement:

> The Utopia Public Library is in the business of providing *young adults* of this town with free access to all of the information they need to lead happy, productive, useful lives. The information is provided through a collection of materials in all formats, expert professional information services, and age-appropriate programs of all kinds.

Vision Statement

PRSPL does not deal with vision statements, but this component has become increasingly common in the planning process since 1987. Unlike the mission statement, which says what the library's business is *now,* the vision statement tries to articulate what the world *will be* like when the mission is accomplished. It is value-laden, optimistic, and uplifting, designed to inspire people with enthusiasm for the organization and its business.

For example, YALSA adopted the following vision statement in 1994:

> In every library in the nation, quality library service to young adults is provided by a staff that understands and respects the unique informational, educational, and recreational needs of teenagers. Equal access to information, services, and materials is recognized as a right not a privilege. Young adults are actively involved in the library decision making process. The library staff collaborates and cooperates with other youth-serving agencies to provide a holistic, community-wide network of activities and services that support healthy youth development.

The YALSA vision statement goes on to list a number of activities in which the organization engages to ensure that the vision becomes a reality.

A vision statement for the Utopia Public Library might be something like this:

> The Utopia Public Library's vision for the community is that, with access to all the information

they need to lead happy, productive, useful lives, the following benefits will result:

All children will enter school ready to learn and will continue to have all the resources they need to learn at their fullest capacity.
Reading will be valued as a life-long source of pleasure, information, and education.
All people will be able to access and evaluate information when they need it, in formats that are appropriate and useful.
The local economic climate will be healthy.
Local government will make wise decisions, with a high degree of participation from its citizenry.
The recreational and cultural life of the community will be stimulating and satisfying, contributing to an excellent overall quality of life for everyone who lives here.

A vision statement for services to young adults at the same library might be something like this:

The Utopia Public Library's vision for the young adults of this community is that, with access to all the information they need to lead happy, productive, useful lives, the following benefits will result:

Young adults will have all the resources they need to learn at their highest capacity.
Reading will be valued as a life-long source of pleasure, information, and education.
All young adults will be able to access and evaluate information when they need it, in formats that are appropriate and useful.
The local economic climate will be healthy. Young adults who want to work will find jobs that are appropriate and rewarding and will have the skills and knowledge needed to be wise consumers.
Local government will make wise decisions, with a high degree of participation from its citizenry, including young adults.
The recreational and cultural life of the community will be stimulating and satisfying, contributing to an excellent overall quality of life for all young adults who live here.

Goals and Objectives

Like vision statements, goals are also future-oriented; they state the results that the library hopes to achieve over the next three to five years. Flowing directly from the roles and mission and vision statements, they provide the framework or outline for setting objectives and action steps. PRSPL points out that a library will probably have both service goals and management goals.

Objectives are the specific short-range, quantifiable results that the library plans to accomplish on its way to achieving its goals. For each goal, the library would typically develop two or three objectives. The goals will remain constant for several years; the objectives will usually be formulated every year, often in connection with the budget cycle.

Following are goals and objectives that might have been developed by the Utopia Public Library. Notice that objectives specific to young adults have been integrated with more-general objectives.

Service Goals

Goal 1: All people in Utopia are able to find solutions to their information needs at the library.

Objectives:

1.1. Increase the Information Transaction Rate from 65 percent to 75 percent by June 30, 19__.
1.2. Increase the Fill Rate to at least 80 percent by June 30, 19__.
1.3. Increase the Children's and Young Adult Homework Fill Rate to at least 80 percent by June 30, 19__.

Goal 2: Reading will be valued by all people in the community as a life-long source of pleasure, education, and entertainment.

Objectives:

2.1. Increase Circulation per Capita, Circulation of Children's Materials per Child, and Circulation of Materials per Young Adult by at least 10 percent by June 30, 19__.
2.2. Provide a minimum of 50 preschool storytimes during the fiscal year ending June 30, 19__.
2.3. Increase enrollment in the Summer Reading Program by 10 percent by August 30, 19__.
2.4. Provide opportunities to participate in book discussion and review groups to at least 50 young adults by June 30, 19__.

Management Goals

Goal 3: The library's physical plant is attractive, comfortable, functional, and safe.

Objectives:

3.1. With input from the Young Adult Advisory Council, remodel Young Adult Corner by June 30, 19__.

3.2. Install fiber-optic cable in work rooms and public areas of the library by June 30, 19__.

Goal 4: The library hires and trains the best people available that are required to accomplish its mission.

Objectives:

4.1. Provide cross-training in age-specific reference and readers' advisory work to all librarians by June 30, 19__.
4.2. Complete audit of five-year staffing needs by December 30, 19__.

Action Steps

This book does not tell you how to develop the action steps necessary to reach your objectives. There are other excellent resources to help you create the mix of services that will excite, inform, educate, and entertain the young adults in your community. Good places to begin include:

Chelton, Mary K., ed. *Excellence in Library Services to Young Adults: The Nation's Top Programs,* Chicago: American Library Association, 1994.
Chelton, Mary K., and James R. Rosinia. *Bare Bones: Young Adult Services Tips for Public Library Generalists.* Chicago: American Library Association, 1993.
Directions for Library Service to Young Adults. 2d ed. Chicago: American Library Association/ Young Adult Library Services Division, 1993.
Jones, Patrick R. *Connecting Young Adults and Libraries: A How-to-Do-It Manual.* New York: Neal-Schuman, 1992.
Wilson-Lingbloom, Evie. *Hangin' Out at Rocky Creek: A Melodrama in Basic Young Adult Services in Public Libraries.* Metuchen, N.J.: Scarecrow, 1994.

The process itself is easy. For each objective, develop realistic action steps. These steps should be specific activities that will help to accomplish the objective. Leave room, however, to be spontaneous and flexible as well. Don't have the year programmed so densely that you are unable to act on a sudden good idea from the young adult advisory council or respond to an unexpected critical need that presents itself. Henry Mintzberg, a leading management scholar, has recently attributed a decline in planning activity in business to the rigidity that some planning processes have produced. You want to be guided by the plan, not imprisoned by it.

Evaluation Strategies

Because you have stated your objectives in quantifiable terms, you have made it possible to measure your progress toward meeting those objectives. Be sure, however, that you make specific plans to evaluate so that data collection actually occurs. Make a time table for data collection. Parts 2 and 3 of this book will help as you get ready to evaluate your plan of library service to young adults.

Sources for Additional Information

Chelton, Mary K., ed. *Excellence in Library Services to Young Adults: The Nation's Top Programs.* Chicago: American Library Association, 1994.
A compilation of the fifty programs for young adults that were selected for recognition by ALA President Hardy Franklin's Committee on Customer Service to Youth.
Chelton, Mary K., and James M. Rosinia. *Bare Bones: Young Adult Services Tips for Public Library Generalists.* Chicago: American Library Association, 1993.
A sensible guide to serving young adults for people who are not young adult librarians.
Directions for Library Services to Young Adults. 2d ed. Chicago: American Library Association/ Young Adult Library Services Association, 1993.
The basic philosophy for library service to young adults as developed by the YALSA.
Greer, Roger C., and Martha L. Hale. "The Community Analysis Process." In *Public Librarianship: A Reader,* edited by Jane Robbins-Carter 358–66. Littleton, Colo.: Libraries Unlimited, 1982.
Describes how to do a community analysis.
Jones, Patrick. *Connecting Young Adults and Libraries: A How-to-Do-It Manual.* New York: Neal-Schuman, 1992.
Everything you need to do to mount an effective program of services for young adults.
———. "Know Your P's and Q's: A Planning Process for Young Adult Programs." *Journal of Youth Services in Libraries* 2 (Fall 1988): 95–100.
Thirty-nine steps to successful young adult programs.
———. "Role Playing: Young Adults as Independent Learners." *Voice of Youth Advocates* 16 (Aug. 1993): 136–40.

An interesting discussion of young adults and the independent learning center role.

McClure, Charles R., et al. *Planning and Role Setting for Public Libraries*. Chicago: American Library Association, 1987.

The general guide to planning for public libraries.

McNeal, James U. *Kids as Customers: A Handbook of Marketing to Children*. New York: Lexington Books, 1992.

Reveals the marketing strategies that have enabled many companies to develop life-long loyalty in customers who started as children.

Metoyer-Duran, Cheryl. "Cross-Cultural Research in Ethnolinguistic Communities: Methodological Considerations." *Public Libraries* 32 (Jan./Feb. 1993): 18–26.

Gives many useful suggestions for doing research in communities where ethnic ties are strong and the dominant language is not English.

———. *Gatekeepers in Ethnolinguistic Communities*. Norwood, N.J.: Ablex, 1993.

While this book is concerned only with adults, it gives valuable insights into information-seeking behavior in ethnolinguistic communities.

Mintzberg, Henry. *The Rise and Fall of Strategic Planning: Reconceiving Roles for Planning, Plans, Planners*. New York: The Free Press, 1994.

A scholarly but readable reconsideration of planning in business.

Walter, Virginia A. "The Information Needs of Children." *Advances in Librarianship* 18 (1994): 111–29.

Focusing on the information needs of ten-year-old children, this research report includes a key informant methodology that could be used as part of a needs assessment with young adults as well.

Weisner, Stan. *Information Is Empowering: Developing Public Library Services for Youth at Risk*. 2d ed. Oakland, Calif.: Bay Area Library and Information System, 1992.

A practical guidebook to planning and implementing programs for a particular segment of the young adult community. Includes useful chapters on conducting needs assessment and involving young adults in the planning process.

Wilson-Lingbloom, Evie. *Hangin' Out at Rocky Creek: A Melodrama in Basic Young Adult Services in Public Libraries*. Metuchen, N.J.: Scarecrow, 1994.

A creative, passionate, and practical guide to providing library services for young adults, this is essential reading for library administrators as well as young adult specialists.

Youth Indicators 1993: Trends in the Well-Being of Youth. Washington, D.C.: U.S. Department of Education, Office of Educational Research and Improvement, National Center for Education Statistics, 1993.

Presents aggregate data about the conditions of young adults in this country, focusing on their lives outside school.

Zinn, Laura. "They're Back: Teens." *Business Week* (11 Apr. 1994): 76–86.

An overview of the demographics and trends that have made teens attractive to marketing experts.

Zweizig, Douglas, et al. *Evaluating Library Programs & Services: TELL IT!* Madison, Wisc.: School of Library and Information Studies, University of Wisconsin–Madison, 1993.

A framework for library planning and evaluation that encompasses *Planning and Role Setting for Public Libraries; Output Measures for Public Libraries,* second edition; and other planning and evaluation techniques. Includes chapters on vision statements and service design.

PART

2

Evaluating the Results: The Measurement Process

Better planning, as described in Part 1, should result in better services for young adults. Through systematic evaluation, you can determine what actually happened as a result of your planning. Evaluation can help you decide if your goals and objectives were met and help you continually to improve your services.

Measurement, Public Libraries, and Service to Young Adults

Measurements provide organizations with management information that is useful in many ways. All organizations use a variety of measurement devices to:

establish baselines or bench marks for current levels of performance
compare past and future levels of performance with the current levels
develop goals and objectives
monitor progress toward achievement of goals and objectives
provide data for decision making
prepare and justify budget requests and resource allocations

Public libraries have always measured some aspects of their operations. From the earliest days in this country, librarians have kept track of circulation and book stock. The measurement efforts sponsored by the Public Library Development Project (PLDP) of the Public Library Association (PLA) represent a new approach, however. Beginning with the first edition of *Output Measures for Public Libraries* in 1982, there has been a movement to refocus public library measurement activities. One goal of these efforts has been to standardize definitions of data elements and data collection techniques to make the data comparable across organizations and over time. Another goal has been to capture in quantifiable data the whole range of outputs that libraries provide, not just circulation and reference, and to present them in a context that is meaningful to decision makers.

PLDP has adopted the systems approach to measurement, distinguishing between the inputs and outputs of a library, conceptualized as a system. With the new emphasis on accountability in local government, budget analysts are increasingly interested in knowing what results (outputs) they are getting for the resources (inputs) they are providing. The output measures developed through the PLDP are intended in part to help librarians show how big a bang taxpayers are getting for their bucks.

A Planning Process for Public Libraries by Vernon Palmour et al. (Chicago: American Library Association, 1980) and *Output Measures for Public Libraries* by Douglas L. Zweizig and Eleanor Jo Rodger (Chicago: American Library Association, 1982) represented important first steps in institutionalizing planning and evaluation techniques in public libraries. When the PLA New Standards Task Force set out to revise them, it adopted the concept of public library roles developed by Lowell Martin and tried to make the output measures more standardized and easier to implement.

The two basic PLDP products currently are *Planning and Role Setting for Public Libraries* (PRSPL) by Charles McClure et al. and *Output Measures for Public Libraries* (OMPL), second edition, by Nancy Van House et al. They were followed by *Output Measures for Public Library Service to Children* by Virginia Walter (Chicago: American Library Association, 1992), which, like this book, shows how the basic output measures can be adapted and enhanced to look at the results of library service to a particular segment of the library user population. All of these manuals support the work of the Public Library Data Service, which collects and publishes in an annual volume comparable data from public libraries throughout the nation.

It is likely that PLA's approach to planning and evaluation will continue to develop. Output measures are also certain to change. At the least, new aspects of library services, such as the use of electronic information technology, will need to be accounted for in new ways.

Government officials are increasingly looking for more-sophisticated measures of results, measures of *outcomes* or impacts, rather than the output measures described in this book. Outcomes look at the effect of organizational outputs on the users of those services. **Circulation per Capita** is an output measure; an outcome measure would look at the impact of circulation on the people checking out the books. Has the literacy rate gone up as a result? How has the quality of life improved for people checking out library books? Do they cook better, more nutritious meals? Make wiser buying decisions? Make more informed judgments about public affairs? Do a better job of parenting? Are they more-effective job seekers and job holders? Are they happier? It is clear that measuring outcomes requires more sophisticated techniques than this book proposes. But that's the next cycle. For now, you can concentrate on measuring outputs. You will need to know the outputs before you can measure outcomes in most cases anyway.

Measurement and the Planning Process

In this book, planning and measurement are closely linked. Measurement is seen as a tool for gathering information about the library and the community that, in turn, feeds into the development of roles, mission, and goals for the library. Output measures are used in formulating the objectives that the library uses as benchmarks to see if it is achieving its goals. Output measures monitor the actual activities that are implemented to achieve those benchmarks.

It should be obvious that, while planning and evaluation seem to be closely and inevitably linked, you can use output measures independently of the planning and role setting process. If you use a different planning process in your library, output measures still can be used to evaluate your progress. Furthermore, output measures can be used in the evaluation of grant-funded programs. They can be used to establish benchmarks for total quality management efforts, and they can be used for budget requests.

Managing the Measurement Process

As you begin to implement a measurement process in your library, you will want to consider a number of factors about your organization, your own position, and the community.

Organizational Considerations

Every library is different. Size, structure, current practices, resources, and organizational culture are going to affect the decisions you make about output measures for service to young adults.

Size

If the library is contained in one building, the choices are relatively simple. You will have to coordinate efforts at only one site. If, however, the library is a part of a multibranch system, there are other decisions to make. Are all agencies going to measure the same things at the same time? Are you going to calculate and report your findings (the output measures) for the system as a whole or for each agency? Do you want to identify the YOUNG ADULT POPULATION OF LEGAL SERVICE AREA for each agency or for the system as a whole? If the boundaries of branch service areas do not correspond with census tracts, it is very difficult to determine the YOUNG ADULT POPULATION OF LEGAL SERVICE AREA for individual branches.

Central libraries present some particular problems when applying per capita measures. If you assume that the central library has its own geographic service area separate from that of the branches and calculate per capita measures based on that service area, its outputs per capita will tend to be very large. On the other hand, if you consider that the central library serves the entire population, then its per capita outputs will tend to be small. In most cases, the central library's legal service area should be defined as the entire population served by the library. Remember the circumstances under which data were gathered when you analyze and interpret the data.

Implementing the measurement effort in a small library tends to be more straightforward than in larger libraries. Larger libraries will require more effort to coordinate a large-scale measurement effort, but they should also have more resources to do the job.

Structure

The structure of an organization is the way in which its functions and staffing relationships are organized or configured. Small libraries will usually have simpler structures than large ones, but virtually all public libraries are bureaucracies with some form of hierarchy, chain of command, and routinized ways of doing things. You will need to consider these aspects of structure as you think about how to implement your output measure effort.

Virtually all of the output measures in this book require cooperation from more than one department of the library. All public service staff, for example, must assist in collecting the data for **Young Adult Information Transaction Completion Rate** during two weeks out of the year. All staff who put on library programs are involved in collecting data all year long for the **Program Attendance per Young Adult** measure. Good working relationships with circulation staff will help facilitate the implementation of the Materials Use measures. Administrative support is required for the whole effort. Be sure at the beginning that you have the support of library administration and that you have good communication procedures in place for coordinating the data collection activities with all concerned staff.

Current Practices

Most libraries already have some measurement practices in place right now. How does the plan for young adult output measures fit with the current practices? If the library currently follows the guidelines in *Output Measures for Public Libraries* and *Output Measures for Library Service to Children* for collecting reference data, for example, you are probably counting reference transactions at least two and possibly three weeks out of the year. Are you going to suggest that the library add two more weeks of data collection to calculate **Young Adult Information Transactions per Young Adult,** or are you going to try to integrate the collection of young adult data with the overall library effort?

Because of the scarcity of existing data about young adult library usage in most libraries, most of the output measures in this book involve instituting special data collection procedures. Even the circulation data, which are available to most libraries for children's and adult materials, are frequently not available for young adult materials or for young adult usage of general library materials. It may be necessary to convince the rest of the library staff that it is important enough to have the data about young adult usage to gain their cooperation in making a special effort to collect it.

Resources

All of the output measures in this book require some extra effort by library staff to implement. You and your library will have to make a commitment to putting time and energy into the project. Because no library has extra staff, you may want to consider using volunteers for data collectors in many measures. Do not be misled into thinking that the use of volunteers frees the staff from expending any effort. On the contrary, volunteers deserve and usually need considerable training, supervision, and reinforcement if they are going to be effective.

In particular, young adult volunteers can be enormously helpful in implementing many of these output measures. They may require close and effective supervision; however, in many cases they are the absolutely right people to do the job. They are easily able to identify other young adults for measures such as **Young Adult Library Visits per Young Adult** or **Young Adult Fill Rate,** which require that young adults be identified by the survey taker. Properly trained, they will see that they have a stake in the results and will be responsible, reliable, enthusiastic workers.

Not only are young adult volunteers often the right people to do the job but involving them in meaningful ways is also the right thing to do. Youth participation is an important value in library service to young adults. Librarians who are youth advocates recognize the library's obligation to provide opportunities for teenagers to build self-esteem, learn job skills, develop a sense of political efficacy, and reap the personal rewards of community service. Most librarians who have worked with young adult volunteers believe that the extra effort is worthwhile. There are a number of useful references in the "Sources for Further Information" section of this chapter that will help you use volunteers of all ages wisely and well.

Organizational Culture

Anthropologists talk about culture as the shared, learned behavior of a people. They study the culture of societies, tribes, and small groups such as street gangs or crews of volunteer fire fighters. Management theorists study the culture of organizations. The values and traditions of organizations are reflected in their cultures. The cultures are reflected in the stories workers and managers tell about their organizations and in the people they describe as organizational heroes and villains. People contemplating organizational change cannot ignore the culture of the organization.

You probably learned something about your library's culture during the planning process. Think about it again as you plan to implement the measurement cycle. Does your organization leap to embrace innovation, or is it slow to change, pointing with pride to traditions of the past? Does it respond most readily to initiatives from the staff, the public, or elected officials? Does it value up-to-the-minute management techniques? Is communication between top management and other staff formal or informal? What kinds of behaviors are rewarded and sanctioned? Does the library see itself as a valued part of the community, or does it have a form of siege mentality, fighting off enemies on all sides? Is morale high or low? Why? An audit of these intangibles that make up the culture will help you develop effective change strategies and communicate more effectively when you need to persuade colleagues, supervisors, and subordinates to participate in the effort to quantify the library's services for young adults.

Scheduling

Many of the output measures in this book involve sampling—collecting data systematically and intensively during two typical weeks during the year, one during summer and one during the school year. You will need to consider carefully how to schedule these two weeks.

The first consideration is that these weeks be truly typical. Weeks that are likely to be unusually busy or unusually slow are not typical weeks. You will not, therefore, select the first week of school because that is likely to be unusually slow. Neither will you select the week in February when every high school student in the community visits the library to do research for Black History Month because that period is likely to be unusually busy. Use good professional judgment, keeping in mind that the goal is to collect the best, most meaningful data that are available.

A second consideration is how to coordinate the collection of young adult data elements with the other data elements that the library needs to gather. While most librarians in the field test sites expressed some concern that young adult data might get lost if they were collected at the same time as the general data, they also felt that it was unlikely that the library would be able to devote another two weeks just to the collection of young adult statistics.

The Ventura County Library pretested the Information Services measures and demonstrated that it was possible to get good data for children's, young adults', and adults' information transactions during the same week. Instructions for gathering all three age-specific statistics during the same week are provided in Part 3, in the section "Information Services Measures." You could probably coordinate the implementation of **Children's Fill Rate** and **Young Adult Fill Rate** during the same weeks, giving the forms to every patron under 18 and then sorting the returns by age. Talk these issues through with your colleagues and coordinate where you can. It will make the level of effort less burdensome and build nice interdepartmental partnerships.

In any case, be sure to allow enough time to plan your data collection. It always takes more time than expected to recruit and train volunteers and communicate with the staff. The bigger the library, the longer the lead time needed. Allow for a pretest of at least a few days to be sure that you have the bugs out of your data collection procedures. And allow enough time between the pretest and the real thing to make adjustments, retrain, and communicate all over again.

Personnel Issues

All of the pretest and field test site librarians agreed that they needed more time than they were given for training and communication. Be sure that *everyone* knows what you are doing and *why* you are doing it. Nobody ever welcomes additional work if they don't know why they are doing it. Keep in mind that even a minimal level of effort doing output measures represents an increase in work for at least some of the staff. Be sure that everyone knows what is expected.

On the other hand, some people involved with the measurement effort may become *too* enthusiastic. They will get caught up in the excitement of counting and develop a kind of "sweeps mentality," inflating the numbers without even thinking about it. Remind everybody that the goal of the project is to get realistic numbers, not the highest numbers. Congratulate people for the rigor with which they collect data, not for the sheer quantity of data they collect.

Plan to be available and visible during the data collection process. Be on hand to answer questions, correct dubious practices, and keep up people's spirits. Keep reminding people how important it is that the library have quantitative evidence accounting for its work with young adults.

Be sure that you communicate the results to everybody when the process is over and you have

calculated the measures. It is discouraging to put in extra work on a project and never hear the outcome. You may want to involve your data collectors in an analysis session, getting their input on how to interpret the numbers. At any rate, have a debriefing session right away to hear firsthand what worked and what didn't work during the data collection phase. Take notes and do it better next time.

Your Position in the Library

Many of you reading this book are not in the top decision-making circles of your library. You will need to be both a good organizational strategist and a credible team player to be effective. Be wary about coming on too strong as a youth advocate in this context. You must be sure that your proposals emphasize benefits that will accrue to the library as a whole as a result of this intensified look at the services for young adults.

Some of you may have been assigned the task of implementing the young adult output measures by the library administration with little or no advance warning or consultation. Take heart; it is not as difficult as it may appear at first, and you will learn some technical evaluation skills that you can apply in many other situations.

Some of you are library administrators who recognize the value of a segmented marketing approach to public library service and who have already become aware of the young adult segment of your user population. I guarantee that taking the time to quantify your work with young adults will produce results that will improve your decision making, impress your elected officials, and perhaps surprise you and your staff.

As a manager, you are aware of the impact that planning and evaluation have on work load; you are also aware of the benefits that the investment of time will bring. Your strong and visible support for well-planned, accountable library services for young adults will make a tremendous difference to staff involved in these activities.

Selecting the Measures to Implement

It is highly unlikely that any library will implement all or even most of these output measures. They are intended as a menu of options.

The library's selection of roles may dictate the young adult output measures you want to implement. The discussion of roles in Part 1 includes suggestions for specific output measures to consider for each of the eight roles. A library with a Reference Center role emphasis, for example, will almost certainly want to think about using the Information Use measures, while one with a Popular Materials Library role will look more closely at the Materials Use and Materials Availability measures.

In addition, the library's current level of emphasis on service to young adults also will influence your decisions. If this is a strong aspect of the library's overall service plan, you will probably implement more of these special output measures than a library with a more limited program for teenagers. If you are thinking about adding or cutting some aspect of service to young adults, these output measures also would help in making the decision and evaluating the consequences. It would be interesting to know, for example, if various young adult use measures increase when you add a young adult librarian or if they decrease when such a position is cut.

The organization's current involvement with general or children's output measures may also influence the decision about which young adult output measures to select. If you are already collecting **Circulation per Capita** and **Children's Circulation per Child,** for example, it may seem reasonable to add **Circulation of Young Adult Materials per Young Adult** and/or **Circulation of Materials per Young Adult** to give a broader picture.

Level of effort is the last internal factor to consider when deciding which young adult output measures to implement. Some of these measures can be implemented with relatively little extra effort; for others, the data collection is quite labor-intensive. If you feel that the level of effort must be minimal, think about implementing those measures for which you already have data, perhaps **Circulation of Young Adult Materials per Young Adult** or those for which the data collection could be absorbed into regular ongoing routines with little effort, such as the **Young Adult Information Transactions per Young Adult.**

Factors outside the library may also influence the selection of specific young adult output measures. Youth initiatives have become increasingly important at all levels of government recently. If the county launches a highly publicized effort to increase after-school activities for young adults or to raise standardized test scores, for example, you may be called on to show what the library is doing in this area. Then you might want to point to your after-school **Building Use by Young Adults, Homework Center Visits by Young Adults,** or **Program Attendance per Young Adult** measures to demonstrate the library's importance in the lives of young people.

Collecting and Analyzing the Data

Part 3 contains specific directions for collecting and analyzing the data for each output measure. However, the following sections present some general issues and guidelines to keep in mind for the process as a whole.

Identifying Young Adults

Many of the output measures require that the data collector be able to identify a young adult by sight. Where feasible, the data collection instructions include additional methods for validating individual observations. For example, signage could be used to prompt customers to volunteer their age group information to reference librarians collecting Information Services statistics. The forms for **Young Adult Fill Rate** have an age line, so forms given to people who are too old or too young can be discarded. Data collectors counting young adults entering the library for **Young Adult Library Visits per Young Adult,** however, must rely on their own observations. Be ready to give the data collectors some guidance.

Before you even begin, be clear about how you are defining a young adult. As noted in the Introduction, regardless of the definition you use, be consistent in your use.

Once you are clear about the age range being counted, give your data collectors some tips. Some clues that other libraries have passed on include observing school uniforms and insignia, checking for car keys, and noting dress and hair styles. Some adult data collectors have found it helpful to have a mental picture of specific young adults that they know. You might ask a group of young adults from ages 12 to 18 to meet with the data collectors and give their own advice. This approach also has the advantage of providing the data collectors with some local, real-life young adults as examples. At the lower end of the age range, boys tend to look very young. At the older end, girls sometimes look much older. The data collectors should not worry too much, however, if they make an occasional mistake in identification. It is likely that for every 19-year-old counted in error, a less physically developed 13-year-old was missed. The results should even out in the end.

To help with consistency, keep an output measures notebook in which you record information such as the library's definition of a young adult, dates selected for "typical week" data collections, problems encountered and solved, and notes about any local variations from the directions given in the manual. If the statistics are to be valid, reliable, and comparable, you must be sure that you measure what you intend to measure and that the same things are counted in the same way by everybody doing the counting, each time that you count. Keep notes of exactly what and how you count each time you do it.

Statistical Methods

The statistical methods used in these young adult output measures are simple descriptive methods. You will not be asked to figure correlations, regressions, or other more complicated calculations. You are not doing hypothesis testing. As Doug Zweizig and his colleagues at the University of Wisconsin–Madison point out, the goal of this work is not to *prove* but to *improve*.

As in OMPL, second edition, and *Output Measures for Public Library Service to Children,* this manual tries to provide standardized definitions and standardized procedures in an effort to help you get results that are valid, reliable, and comparable. If you follow the directions, you should get results that are good enough to allow you to use them as quantitative indicators of the library's outputs in specific areas.

A *valid* measurement is one that measures what it says it measures. For example, a valid **Young Adult Information Transactions per Young Adult** measures *all* reference and readers' advisory questions asked by *all* young adult library users. It does not measure questions that fall outside the category of reference and readers' advisory questions. However, it does include queries made over the telephone as well as in person. It counts *all* questions asked by young adults and does not count questions asked by children or adults unless it is clear that a young adult is the intended end user of the information sought. The particular parameters must be understood by all data collectors.

Data collectors who understand the parameters of the phenomenon they are counting will also contribute to the reliability of the measure. A *reliable* measure is one that is counted the same way by everybody doing the counting. Try to ensure reliability by giving all data collectors the same training, by giving as many guidelines as possible, and by monitoring the data collection to be sure that dubious practices are modified. At one field test site, for example, the supervising librarian discovered that two pages assigned to take the building use count each hour on the hour were starting five minutes early if there seemed to be a lot of young adults around. They wanted to be sure that the young adults didn't slip away before they were counted. The reliability of the measure was threatened by their failure to start the count at exactly the same time for each collection period.

Comparability means that the same things are measured in the same way each time you collect the data. If you are scrupulous about consistency in procedures and definitions each time you collect data for a specific output measure, you will be able to compare the results and observe trends. If conditions change for some reason, you must make note of this change and allow for the changes when you interpret the results. For example, a change in library hours may affect **Young Adult Library Visits per Young Adult.**

Sampling

Almost all of the output measures in this book involve some sort of sampling. *Sampling* means that you do not count every item in the universe of data elements, but rather in a representative piece of the universe. Most measures do not require that you collect data for the entire year, for example. Instead, you select two sample weeks, two typical or representative weeks out of the year—one in summer and one during the school year—in which to collect the data. Then you generalize from those sample weeks to indicate an annual figure. The calculations include a formula for weighting the school year week more heavily than the summer week because the school year is approximately three times longer than summer.

For those sample weeks, it is best that you collect data during all the hours the library is open. If staffing limitations make this recommendation impossible, however, you can "sample the sample" by selecting representative hours out of the week in which to collect data. The goal in selecting the typical weeks and the sample hours is to select time periods that represent the whole.

You want to avoid sample bias, where the sample is *not* representative of the whole. If you select a sample week during the school year in which usage is heavier than usual, you will bias your sample and produce results that are suspect. You should select your sample hours during the week with the same care so that they are representative of the whole. If the library is open two mornings a week, then morning hours must be included among the sample times, even though you suspect that not many young adults use the library at those times.

Table 1 is an example of a sampling schedule for a library that is open Monday through Thursday from 10 A.M. to 9 P.M. and Friday and Saturday from 10 A.M. to 6 P.M.

Table 2 is a sampling schedule for a library that is open Monday and Wednesday from 1 P.M. to 9 P.M. and Tuesday, Thursday through Saturday from 10 A.M. TO 6 P.M.

You must also think about sample size. The rule of thumb is that you must have at least 100 items in the sample to achieve acceptable tolerance and confidence levels. After this, you need to have 400 items to achieve significantly greater tolerance and confidence levels. If your sample has been well-chosen, you really do not need more data than this to project your findings to the population as a whole.

In practice, you must be able to tally at least 100 young adult information transactions or collect at least 100 survey forms during each of the two sample weeks to calculate an output measure for the whole year. If the library is not busy enough to produce that level of activity, consider extending each sample period to two weeks to get usable data.

Interpreting the Results

For each output measure Part 3 provides some specific suggestions for interpreting the findings. This section is a more general discussion of interpretation issues. It is sometimes tempting when you first produce some usable data and calculate the output measures to make more claims than the evidence really warrants. Keep in mind that these are simple quantitative measures, telling you "how many" of something in relation to "how many" of something else. You will need to look elsewhere to find answers to the interesting questions, "why?" or "how?" or "so what?"

Keep the numbers in perspective. Numbers are important in demonstrating accountability. They are useful for comparing things. The problem is that they can take on a life of their own. Sometimes the process of counting widgits becomes more important than the widgits themselves. Remember that you are in the business of providing library services, not the business of counting outputs. Don't let measurement become an end in itself. You are counting only to help evaluate how well you are providing those library services.

The very process of counting something can lead to a kind of halo effect in which the something gets bigger or more numerous just because it is being counted. It is also easy to fall into the trap of assuming that big numbers are better than little numbers. Not all young adult output mea-

Time	Mon.	Tues.	Wed.	Thurs.	Fri.	Sat.
10–11 A.M.	DATA		DATA			DATA
11–12 A.M.		DATA		DATA		DATA
12–1 P.M.					DATA	DATA
1–2 P.M.		DATA		DATA		DATA
2–3 P.M.	DATA		DATA			DATA
3–4 P.M.		DATA		DATA	DATA	DATA
4–5 P.M.	DATA		DATA			DATA
5–6 P.M.		DATA				DATA
6–7 P.M.				DATA		XXXX
7–8 P.M.	DATA		DATA			XXXX
8–9 P.M.		DATA		DATA		XXXX

Table 1. Sampling Schedule

Time	Mon.	Tues.	Wed.	Thurs.	Fri.	Sat.
10–11 A.M.	XXXX	DATA	XXXX			DATA
11–12 A.M.	XXXX		XXXX		DATA	DATA
12–1 P.M.	XXXX		XXXX	DATA		DATA
1–2 P.M.	DATA	DATA			DATA	DATA
2–3 P.M.			DATA			DATA
3–4 P.M.	DATA	DATA		DATA		DATA
4–5 P.M.					DATA	DATA
5–6 P.M.		XXXX		DATA		DATA
6–7 P.M.		XXXX	DATA	XXXX	XXXX	XXXX
7–8 P.M.	DATA	XXXX		XXXX	XXXX	XXXX
8–9 P.M.			DATA	XXXX	XXXX	XXXX

Table 2. Sampling Schedule

sures will yield big numbers. **Young Adult Participation Rate,** for example, will tend to show that a very small percentage of the total young adult population is involved in voluntary service at the library. This finding is not surprising. In *Volunteering and Giving, 1992* (Washington, D.C.: Independent Sector, 1993), the authors report that in 1991, 61 percent of teenagers between the ages of 12 and 17 participated in volunteer activities in all kinds of organizations. Of those young adults, 29 percent volunteered for religious organizations, and another 25 percent were involved in extracurricular school activities. The remaining 46 percent (of the 61 percent who volunteered) spread their service throughout a variety of organizations and activities, public libraries among them. While youth participation is not the primary function of any public library, many libraries try to make opportunities for participation available to young adults. Those libraries would collect data and calculate **Young Adult Participation Rate** not with the expectation of seeing a high number but rather of comparing the results over time.

None of the PLDP output measures manuals will tell you "how high is high" or what is "too low." The output measures are part of an effort to move away from quantitative standards that all libraries must meet. The output measures are intended to provide baseline data that allow decision makers to measure progress toward goals and to see trends developing. You must decide in your own situation what quantitative goals you want to achieve and what kind of value judgment you will make about each output measure.

Numbers, of course, whether high or low, do not tell the whole story by themselves. Many important things go on in libraries that resist quantifying. Sometimes the story of one individual whose life was changed through an interaction with a library is worth more than any number of output measures. Anecdotal evidence, collected as you provide library service to young adults, can enrich your understanding of the numbers. You may wish to keep a journal handy in your desk to record specific examples of small victories and tender triumphs that make your work so rewarding. These journal entries can help bring the numbers alive when you report the results.

Using Qualitative Evaluation Methods

Quantitative research methods require you to assign numbers to things. Qualitative methods, on the other hand, allow you to acquire empirical evidence of more subjective phenomena, such as opinions, attitudes, and feelings. Qualitative data can be used in an evaluation process in a variety of ways:

- They can help to clarify or identify issues before developing a quantitative research design. For example, you might interview school library media specialists in the community before you

decide whether to implement a **Young Adult Homework Fill Rate**. By providing insights about the limitations or strengths of their own resources, school specialists could help you understand the potential use of public library resources for homework purposes.

- Qualitative data can help clarify quantitative research findings. You might conduct focus groups with young adults to try to understand why **Young Adult Library Visits per Young Adult** suddenly increased or decreased dramatically.
- Qualitative data can add an important interpretive dimension to the reporting of quantitative data. You might add pertinent quotes from young adults who serve on your young adult advisory council to the library's annual report to show why the library cares about its **Young Adult Participation Rate**.

There are many ways to collect qualitative data, including structured observations, participant observations, in-depth interviews, and focus groups, and there are many good resources from which you can learn more about them. Some are listed in the Sources for Additional Information section at the end of this part. Two of the most useful and feasible techniques for obtaining qualitative data are interviews and focus groups. Brief discussions of these methods follow.

Interviews

Interviewing is a way of getting information from individuals by asking them questions. Many librarians use interview techniques every day when they try to find out what information patrons really want at the reference desk. Some interviews are little more than oral surveys, getting quick answers to closed-end questions. The kind of interviews that tend to yield richer qualitative data are sometimes called in-depth interviews.

In-depth interviews tend to be longer than surveys, lasting at least half an hour. The interviewer starts with a carefully prepared list of open-ended questions but feels free to ask follow-up questions or to follow new lines of inquiry that open up as the interview proceeds.

Selecting Interview Subjects

Interviewing key informants can provide important community information. Key informants are carefully selected individuals who are presumed to have special knowledge about a particular subject. They are not part of a random sample, but rather people who are chosen for their particular expertise. In a "snowball" research design, you might start with only two or three identified key informants. By asking each of them for more names of people to talk to, the number of subjects increases in much the way that a snowball grows as you roll it in the snow.

For evaluation purposes, you usually want to talk to people who use the service or program that you are evaluating. Some examples would be frequent users of the homework center, young adults who regularly attend programs, "typical" users of your reference services or materials collection, young adult volunteers, or young adult advisory council members. Just as with your selection of typical weeks in which to collect data, the selection of interview subjects should aim to find users who are as representative as possible. It is often tempting to interview the young adults that you know the best, but they may not be the most typical young adult library users. Try for more of a cross section of interview subjects.

How Many People to Interview

The answer to the question "How many people should you interview?" is "As many as it takes." If you sense that the issues are complex and varied or that there will be many points of view, you should probably try to talk to a broad spectrum of people. In most cases, however, you will probably have a fairly limited number of subjects. Even talking to two or three people in a systematic, in-depth interview will tell you more than you knew before conducting the interviews.

If you are trying to get a sense of what the whole population of young adult library users (or nonusers) thinks about the library or a particular library service, try to interview one representative of each major category in the population. Be sure to include both genders, younger teens as well as older ones, representatives of all ethnic or racial groups, and representatives of significant economic strata or life style groups if appropriate.

Preparing the Questions

You should have some prepared questions even for open-ended interviews. The list of questions is sometimes referred to as the interview schedule. If the list of questions is too short, unless they are unusually provocative questions, you may find that the interview is over too soon. If the list is too long, the subject may get tired of answering the questions. Generally, five or six good questions, with follow-up questions, is the right number.

The questions should be open-ended. That is, they should be the kind of questions that have no predetermined response. Specifically, they should not be the kind of question that results in a short "yes" or "no" answer. For example, "Do you ever check out videos when you come to the library?" is a closed-ended question. "What kinds of things do you check out to take home with you when you come to the library?" is an open-ended question. "Tell me what you do when you come to the library" is even more open and may, in fact, invoke too broad a range of responses to be useful.

The questions should be clear. The subjects may get tense or uncomfortable if they don't understand the questions. Use nontechnical language that your subjects understand. It is all right to clarify if you see that your subject doesn't understand you, but you should try to have questions that speak for themselves.

It is always a good idea to pretest the questions. It will help you discover whether they are as clear as you think they are. The responses also will help you see whether the questions are open-ended. For example, "How satisfied are you with the homework center?" sounds like an open-ended question. It is certainly better than, "Are you satisfied with the homework center?" However, it assumes a degree of satisfaction. What if the young adult is not satisfied at all? A better wording would be, "What do you think about the homework center?" Follow up with narrower questions, such as, "How would you improve it?" or "What do you find most useful about it?" Pretesting will also help you decide on the best sequence of questions.

Appendix A contains some sample interview schedules that you might adapt for evaluating homework center use and user satisfaction with a young adult materials collection.

Conducting the In-Depth Interview

After deciding whom you want to interview and what you want to ask and pretesting your questions, you are ready to schedule interviews. If you are interviewing young adults, check to see if there is a local policy about parental permission.

Schedule the interview at a time that is convenient for the subject and in a neutral place where he or she will feel comfortable. It should be private enough to protect confidentiality but not so private that the subject might feel trapped with the interviewer, a particularly important concern for some young adults. A library meeting room is often a good location. Provide a comfortable chair. While most young adults usually prefer to sit in easy chairs, they often prefer to sit at a table or desk during an interview. It seems to provide a little distance or protection, and it provides the interviewer with a surface on which to take notes or place the tape recorder.

If the subject is a regular library user, you probably don't need to establish rapport. Do be sure, however, to tell the subject again the reason for the interview. You might say something like, "I'm trying to find out what young adults think about the new homework center." If the subject is a stranger, take a few minutes to get acquainted. Exchange names. Tell where you're from or what your job is. Find out a little about the subject. Talking about the weather can help the interviewee feel comfortable at the beginning. Keep it casual. Reassure the subject that there are no right or wrong answers and that your feelings won't be hurt if the subject says something that is critical. Let your interviewee know that you don't intend to ask anything embarrassing or sensitive, but that if you do so accidentally, he or she should not hesitate to point out the problem. The subject always has the right to choose not to answer any question.

Tell the subject that you have five or six broad questions to ask, but there might be some follow-up questions. Give an idea of about how long the interview might take. Be alert to signs that the subject is getting bored or restless or uncomfortable. Don't hesitate to cut the interview short if it is not productive.

Most young adults don't mind being taped. Taping the interview leaves you free from taking notes and provides you with a record of the subject's actual words. This method is desirable if you have the time to transcribe the tape or even listen to it later. If you know that you will never have the time to do anything with the tape, however, it doesn't make sense to tape the interview.

Much of the success of the interview depends on the quality of your listening skills. It can be tremendously empowering and satisfying to the ego to have someone really listen to what you say and to be genuinely interested. As an interviewer, you can communicate your interest and willingness to listen in a number of ways. Sometimes eye contact with the subject is encouraging. Many young adults are quite shy or self-conscious, however, and they may talk more freely if you pay more attention to your notebook. An occasional remark such as "I see," or even "uh-huh" will communicate that you are paying attention. Active listening techniques such as rephrasing the subject's statements from time to time will help to convince him or her that you are really listening and understanding. Avoid the temptation to start talking yourself. Don't yawn.

At the end of most interviews, it is a good idea to ask the usual all-purpose "Is there anything else you'd like to tell me that will help me understand what we're talking about?" Many young adults will just say, "No, not really." Ask one more time, "Are you sure? I'm a good listener." Sometimes the best information will pour out then. Just end the interview at this point, of course, if the subject has nothing else to say. Be sure to thank your subject for providing valuable information.

Analyzing the Interview Data

As soon as possible after an in-depth interview, try to replay the tape or look at the notes again. Write down observations or highlight notes that are particularly interesting. Document anything about the subject's behavior or appearance that affected the interview or your understanding of the information that was shared. For example, note if the subject seemed nervous or confident or suspicious. Summarize the major themes or patterns in the content of the interview.

After interviewing all the subjects, look for differences and points of comparison among the interviewees, as well as for overall patterns. Summarize as major findings the significant information that you learned. Document as evidence actual quotes from the subjects, perhaps with notations about the number of times that a particular opinion or statement was heard from different subjects.

Focus Groups

Focus groups are really nothing more than group interviews. Much of the information about in-depth interviews also applies to focus groups.

The critical difference between interviews and focus groups is that the latter involves group dynamics. This factor can produce an exciting synergy in the group as people are reminded of things they want to say by the comments of others. Once people begin to talk, the results can be unusually rich.

With young adults, peer pressure can work for or against you in focus groups. It is difficult to predict how it will affect a particular group. You can minimize the negative effects by being alert to the relationships of people in the group, by establishing a climate of respect and trust in the group, and by being perceived yourself as someone who genuinely wants to know the opinion of each person there. Your own sincerity and integrity are your best assets. You do not want to put yourself in the position of being an adult that the teenagers want to con.

You can also minimize negative group dynamics by asking questions that the young adults find interesting. Talking about the library could be perceived as being very boring. Phrasing the questions in new ways or putting a fresh spin on them will keep the young adults engaged. For example, instead of asking, "What do you think of the appearance of the young adult area?" you might say, "What word best describes the appearance of the young adult area?" If a spontaneous discussion does not result, follow up with "Why?" or "What do you mean exactly by 'gnarly' or 'boring' (or whatever the responses had been)?"

Appendix A includes a tested set of questions you could use with a focus group of young adult volunteers. Many of the interview questions also could be used in a focus group setting.

The usual rule of thumb in focus group research is to conduct sessions until you can predict the answers you will hear. Four sessions are almost always enough. A single focus group can yield interesting data, but it runs the risk of being a special case. You should always plan on conducting at least two focus groups so you can check for the recurring themes and issues that become your findings.

When you have completed your focus groups, analyze the data as suggested for the in-depth interviews. The findings are those points that emerge most saliently and most frequently. The evidence is the words of the participants.

In both focus groups and interviews, it is possible that your subjects will tell you what they think you want to hear. There is also the possibility that you will subconsciously lead the discussion in directions that favor your interests. You can minimize this tendency by trying very self-consciously to be objective and by using the wording suggested in Appendix A that urges subjects to be candid. It is even better to take yourself out of a research environment in which you have a vested interest. Perhaps you could arrange with another librarian in a nearby location to exchange interview or focus group responsibilities. Trade four focus groups at the other library for four focus groups conducted by your colleague at your site.

More guidance about conducting focus groups may be found in *Output Measures for Public Library Service to Children* by Virginia A. Walter (Chicago: American Library Association, 1992) as well as in several titles in the Sources for Further Information at the end of this part.

Acting on the Results

Remember that when you have finished the data collection and calculated the measure, you have really only begun the process for which the output measures were designed. Now you must act on the results. Some specific courses of action are suggested for each of the young adult output measures. In all cases, you must do *something,* even if it is to consciously continue to do what you are doing now.

Report what you have learned to the data collectors, library staff and administration, elected officials, local newspapers, and the library press. Librarians at a branch library in Long Beach, California, were so excited about the results of their **Building Use by Young Adults** survey that they shared them immediately with the local city councilwoman. Politicians love getting good news, and this information provided a good, natural opportunity to keep the public library in the forefront of the city councilwoman's attention. In Winter Park, Florida, the library director involved the trustees in the planning for field testing various young adult library use measures. As a result, they became interested in applying the results from their planning to a new young adult area in the library. In Fort Wayne, Indiana, a librarian took one of the survey forms for the **Young Adult Fill Rate** that included some particularly nice comments about the staff, made an enlarged copy, and posted it in the staff room.

Discuss the results with various stakeholders. Talk about what they mean. Celebrate if the results warrant it. Take corrective actions if the results show disappointing performance.

Sources for Additional Information

Baker, Sharon L., and F. Wilfrid Lancaster. *The Measurement and Evaluation of Library Services,* 2d ed. Arlington, Va.: Information Resources Press, 1991.

A basic guide to measurement techniques for all kinds of libraries.

Brudney, Jeffrey L. *Fostering Volunteer Programs in the Public Sector: Planning, Initiating, and Managing Volunteer Activities.* San Francisco: Jossey-Bass, 1990.

An excellent overview of the issues involved in managing public sector volunteer programs.

Childers, Thomas A., and Nancy A. Van House. *What's Good? Describing Your Public Library's Effectiveness.* Chicago: American Library Association, 1993.

How to use outcome measures for public libraries.

Conrad, Dan, and Diane Hedin. "School-Based Community Service: What We Know from Research and Theory." *Phi Delta Kappan* 72 (June 1991): 743–9.

The rationale for secondary school community service programs.

Curzon, Susan Carol. *Managing Change: A How-to-Do-It Manual for Planning, Implementing, and Evaluating Change in Libraries*. New York: Neal-Schuman, 1989.

An effective library manager presents practical ideas for implementing organizational change.

Evaluating Youth Participation: A Guide for Program Operators. New York: The National Commission on Resources for Youth, 1982.

Out of print and difficult to find, this guide can provide valuable assistance if you are emphasizing youth participation.

Greenbaum, Thomas L. *The Practical Handbook and Guide to Focus Group Research*. Lexington, Mass.: Lexington, 1988.

Intended primarily for market researchers, this handbook offers good information on conducting focus groups with children and young adults.

Hedin, Diane, and Dan Conrad. *Youth Services: A Guide Book for Developing and Operating Effective Programs*. Washington, D.C.: Independent Sector, 1987.

How to develop effective programs in any organizational setting.

Hutton, Bruce, and Suzanne Walters. "Focus Groups: Linkages to the Community." *Public Libraries* 27 (Fall 1988): 149–52.

How one public library system used focus groups to collect data for a community analysis.

Ihrig, Alice B. *Decision-Making for Public Libraries*. Hamden, Conn.: Library Professional Publications, 1989.

This guidebook for trustees is a good overview for anyone working in libraries.

Ilsley, Paul J. *Enhancing the Volunteer Experience: New Insights on Strengthening Volunteer Participation, Learning and Commitment*. San Francisco: Jossey-Bass, 1990.

Advice for professionals who supervise adult volunteers.

Krueger, Richard A. *Focus Groups: A Practical Guide for Applied Research*. Newbury Park, Calif.: Sage, 1988.

Describes the use of focus group evaluations.

Leather, Deborah J. "How the Focus Group Technique Can Strengthen the Development of a Building Program." *Library Administration and Management* 4 (Spring 1990): 92–5.

How to use focus groups to gather data for a library building program.

Lynch, Mary Jo. "Measurement of Public Library Activity: The Search for Practical Methods." *Wilson Library Bulletin* 57 (Jan. 1983): 388–93.

An informative historical overview of public library measurement efforts.

———. "Public Library Planning: A New Approach." *Library Journal* 105 (15 May 1980): 1131–4.

A look at the origins of the current public library planning process.

McClure, Charles R., et al. *Planning and Role Setting for Public Libraries: A Manual of Options and Procedures*. Chicago: American Library Association, 1987.

One of the basic documents of the Public Library Development Program.

Patton, Michael Quinn. *How to Use Qualitative Methods in Evaluation*. 2d ed. Newbury Park, Calif.: Sage, 1987.

A good general guide, with a particularly good chapter on interviews.

Slonim, Morris. *Sampling in a Nutshell*. New York: Simon and Schuster, 1960.

For anyone who wants to know more about sampling.

Swisher, Robert, and Charles R. McClure. *Research for Decision-Making*. Chicago: American Library Association, 1984.

A source for survey and sampling techniques especially for libraries.

Van House, Nancy, et al. *Output Measures for Public Libraries: A Manual of Standardized Procedures*. 2d ed. Chicago: American Library Association, 1987.

The general manual for overall library services.

Volunteering and Giving among American Teenagers 12 to 17 Years of Age: Findings from a National Survey. Washington, D.C.: Independent Sector, 1992.

A statistical analysis and overview of two dimensions of youth participation.

Walter, Virginia A. "Evaluating Library Services and Programs." In Kathleen Staerkel, Mary Fellowes, and Sue Nespacca, eds., *Youth Services Librarians as Managers: A How-to-Guide from Budgeting to Personnel,* 51–62. Chicago: American Library Association, 1995.

Discusses total quality management and program evaluation as well as the use of output measures.

———. *Output Measures for Public Library Service to Children: A Manual of Standardized Procedures*. Chicago: American Library Association, 1992.

The first effort to apply the general public

library output measures to a particular age-defined segment of the library service population.

Youth Participation in Libraries: It Works. Chicago: American Library Association / Young Adult Library Services Association, 1995.

Guidelines for librarians who advocate and implement youth participation in libraries.

PART

3

The Output Measures

This section of the manual contains directions for each of the output measures organized by type of service. Each measure is calculated from specific data elements, some of which are used in more than one measure. Form 6, Young Adult Data Elements, is a listing of all the data elements used in these young adult output measures. It allows you to keep track of raw numbers in one convenient form. You will probably not collect all data elements in your library, but there is space to record the ones that you do.

As with *Output Measures for Public Libraries,* second edition, and *Output Measures for Public Library Service to Children,* the measures themselves are printed in bold type and data elements are capitalized. For example, the measure **Young Adult Library Visits per Young Adult** is calculated by dividing the data element ANNUAL NUMBER OF LIBRARY VISITS BY YOUNG ADULTS by the data element YOUNG ADULT POPULATION OF LEGAL SERVICE AREA.

The same format is used for each measure:

- A capsule summary of the measure, including a definition, a brief description of how it is calculated, a brief description of the data collection methodology, and an example
- Instructions for collecting the data
- Suggestions for interpreting and using the data
- Pointers and special considerations, if appropriate
- Ideas for further possibilities

Part 3 is a manual and guide to the output measures themselves. Refer back to Part 2 for a more general discussion of the issues involved in implementing them.

Important Definitions

There are three terms that are used throughout the output measures: young adult, YOUNG ADULT POPULATION OF LEGAL SERVICE AREA, and typical week. Please read the following section carefully so you will understand how these terms are used in this manual.

Use of the term *young adult* is discussed extensively in the introduction to this book. For the purposes of output measures, you should follow local custom in defining young adult library customers. It is important that you be consistent in your definition of this age range and that you not overlap with your definitions of either children or adults.

The YOUNG ADULT POPULATION OF LEGAL SERVICE AREA is the data element that is the basic building block of almost all the young adult output measures. It is used to calculate per capita figures. In this manual, *per young adult* means per young adult capita.

The *legal service area* is the geographical area for which the library offers its services and from which the library derives its income. This definition also could include a geographic area that contracts with the library to provide service. The legal service area may be a city, town, county, assessment district, or parts of one or more of these.

The YOUNG ADULT POPULATION OF LEGAL SERVICE AREA is the number of people whom you have defined as young adults who live in the legal service area. If the legal service area corresponds to census tracts, it will be relatively easy to find the population figures for young adults from census data. Other possible sources for population data include

State and local planning agencies
School districts
County and City Data Book
Donnelly Demographics, an online database

The per capita ratio allows you to see how a particular data element, such as ANNUAL CIRCULATION OF LIBRARY MATERIALS TO YOUNG ADULTS or ANNUAL NUMBER OF YOUNG ADULT INFORMATION TRANSACTIONS relates to the young adult population. It makes the data element more meaningful. It is difficult to know how to interpret an ANNUAL NUMBER OF YOUNG ADULT INFORMATION TRANSACTIONS by itself. Putting it into the context of the YOUNG ADULT POPULATION OF LEGAL SERVICE AREA gives it a frame of reference. For example, an ANNUAL NUMBER OF YOUNG ADULT INFORMATION TRANSACTIONS figure of 1,500 in a community in which the YOUNG ADULT POPULATION OF LEGAL SERVICE AREA is 300 results in a **Young Adult Information Transactions per Young Adult** rate of 5. On average, each young adult in this community made 5 requests for reference or readers' advisory assistance during a given year. In a larger community, where the YOUNG ADULT POPULATION OF LEGAL SERVICE AREA is 1,000, the same ANNUAL NUMBER OF YOUNG ADULT INFORMATION TRANSACTIONS figure results in a **Young Adult Information Transactions per Young Adult** rate of 1.5. On average, each young adult in this community asked between 1 and 2 reference or readers' advisory questions during the previous year.

Many of the measures instruct you to collect data during a typical week in summer and a typical week during the school year. The discussion on sampling in Part 2 offers advice on selecting these typical weeks. The rationale for having two typical weeks for data collection for young adult output measures, rather than just one typical week as the manual for general output measures directs, is that young adult usage varies considerably during these two time periods. Curriculum needs tend to dominate during the school year, contributing to heavier use of information services and the general nonfiction collection. Summer is often a more relaxed time for young adult services, with greater emphasis on leisure reading or programming. Because the school year is approximately three times longer than the summer months, the calculations give three times more weight to the data collected during the school year.

In communities where the schools have year-round schedules, librarians should consider whether there is still some equivalent to school term and summer, or nonschool, periods. Some year-round schedules are staggered, with a portion of students in session at all times. Other year-round schedules spread the "off" times throughout the year, with all students off term at the same time. Consider how the local situation affects your data collection. Some libraries divide the year into four quarters and collect data during a typical week during each quarter. They then adjust the calculations so that each week's data carries equal weight.

Library Use Measures

Library Use Measures indicate the actual use of the library building and its facilities.

Young Adult Library Visits per Young Adult is adapted from the general measure in OMPL, second edition. It measures the number of young adults who enter the library building at any time for any purpose during the year.

Building Use by Young Adults indicates the average number of young adults who are in the library at any one time. It enables you to see patterns of use during different time periods.

Furniture/Equipment Use by Young Adults measures the proportion of time, on average, that any particular piece of library furniture or equipment is likely to be in use by a young adult. When calculated, it is expressed in terms of the specific piece of equipment being used, e.g., **Online Public Access Catalog Use per Young Adult.**

Both **Furniture/Equipment Use by Young Adults** and **Building Use by Young Adults** were adapted from measures developed for *Measuring Academic Library Performance: A Practical Approach* by Nancy A. Van House, Beth T. Weil, and Charles McClure (Chicago: American Library Association, 1990). They were also included in *Output Measures for Public Library Service to Children,* and many public libraries have found them useful for giving a richer picture of library usage for children and for staffing and building-planning decisions.

Homework Center Visits per Young Adult is a new measure designed to track use by young adults of a special educational service provided by more and more public libraries in the last few years. Its data collection technique is the same as that for **Young Adult Library Visits per Young Adult.**

Young Adult Library Visits per Young Adult

Definition:	Number of library visits by young adults during the year relative to the number of young adults living in the community served.
Calculation:	ANNUAL NUMBER OF LIBRARY VISITS BY YOUNG ADULTS divided by YOUNG ADULT POPULATION OF LEGAL SERVICE AREA.
Data Collection:	Count young adults entering the library building during one week in summer and one week during the school year; project for a yearly figure.
Example:	During one sample week in summer, 74 young adults entered the library. During one sample week during the school year, 112 young adults entered the library. Multiply 74 by 12 to find Summer Young Adult Visits; the result is 888. Multiply 112 by 40 to find School Year Young Adult Visits; the result is 4,480. Add the Summer Young Adult Visits (888) and the School Year Young Adult Visits (4,480) to find the ANNUAL NUMBER OF LIBRARY VISITS BY YOUNG ADULTS; the total is 5,368. There are 743 young adults who live in this community. Divide the ANNUAL NUMBER OF LIBRARY VISITS BY YOUNG ADULTS (5,368) by the YOUNG ADULT POPULATION OF LEGAL SERVICE AREA (743) to find the **Young Adult Library Visits per Young Adult** measure. The result is 7.2. On average, each young adult in this community visited the library 7.2 times during the year.

$$\frac{(74 \times 12) + (112 \times 40)}{743} = 7.2$$

Collecting the Data

1. Choose a typical week in summer and a typical week during the school year to collect the data.
2. Decide to count all young adult library users entering the library during the sample period or to sample "typical" hours during the sample week. If possible, take the count during all open hours. However, if staffing constraints make this approach impossible, you may select typical hours and use Form 7, Young Adult Library Visits Sampling Work Sheet to calculate your total for the week. Refer to the discussion of sampling in Part 2 for suggestions about setting up a sampling schedule.
3. Some libraries are not open for regular library service during the mornings but do make their facilities available for scheduled class visits during this time. If the library follows this

practice, be sure to consider this fact in determining your "typical" hours or in taking your count. In other words, if the library regularly hosts visits from schools or other youth groups during closed hours, be sure that these visits are also counted.

4. During all scheduled hours, have someone monitor each entrance to the library and tally young adult library users as they enter the library. Volunteers may be drafted to perform this duty. It is best if the counters have no other responsibility during their shift.
5. The people doing the counting may need some guidance about how to identify young adults. Be prepared to cover identification tips in your training.
6. Be sure that all staff is aware that the count is being taken and the reason for the count. They should be prepared to answer questions from library patrons who are curious about the person standing at the door with a clipboard.
7. It is also a good idea to put up signs at strategic locations to announce that a count of young adult library users is being taken.
8. Remind data collectors to count groups as well as individuals. They should count young adults who enter the library *for any reason* and for any length of time.
9. Use Form 8, Young Adult Library Visits Tally Sheet, to keep track of the count. Some libraries want to know how usage varies by the hour. They could design a more detailed form, broken down by time period. All that is needed for the output measure, however, is a daily count if you are counting during all open hours.
10. Some libraries have also found it useful to circle the hash marks that represent groups. Figure 2 is an example of a completed Young Adult Library Visits Tally Sheet.

Calculating the Measure

1. At the end of the sample week, simply count all visits or complete Form 7, Young Adult Library Visits Sampling Work Sheet. Figure 3 is an example of a completed Young Adult Library Visits Sampling Work Sheet. Calculate the appropriate measure. For School Year Young Adult Library Visits, multiply the total number of young adult visits during the week by 40. For Summer Young Adult Library Visits, multiply by 12.
2. Add the two counts together to find the ANNUAL NUMBER OF LIBRARY VISITS BY YOUNG ADULTS .
3. Divide the ANNUAL NUMBER OF LIBRARY VISITS BY YOUNG ADULTS by the YOUNG ADULT POPULATION OF LEGAL SERVICE AREA to get the **Young Adult Library Visits per Young Adult** measure.

Interpreting and Using the Data

1. The **Young Adult Library Visits per Young Adult** measure only tells you how many young adults have entered the library during a given year relative to the number of young adults who live in the community. It tells, *on average,* how many times during the year each young adult in the community came to the library.
2. The number may be less than one. For example, if the ANNUAL NUMBER OF LIBRARY VISITS BY YOUNG ADULTS is 1,000, and 2,000 young adults live in your community, the **Young Adult Library Visits per Young Adult** is 0.5. This figure is somewhat more difficult to express in a meaningful way. Statistically, it means that on average, each young adult in the community came to the library half a time, which might raise the logical question, "How do you visit the library half a time?" It certainly indicates that not every young adult visited the library during the year. You could say, however, that on the average, half of the young adults in the community visited the library during the past year.
3. If you want to increase **Young Adult Library Visits per Young Adult,** you could:

    - Reconsider the mix of programs and services you are offering. Do they meet the needs and interests of young adults in your community?
    - Reevaluate your materials collection. Does it meet the needs and interests of young adults in your community?
    - Look at staff interactions with young adults. Are teenagers made to feel welcome and wanted in the library? Do they receive competent, friendly service?
    - Publicize your services more effectively. Do young adults know what services, programs, and resources you offer for them?
    - Evaluate the physical facility. Is it attractive and inviting to young adults?

Library/Entrance Main Date October 16, 1995

Use one tally sheet each day per entrance. Enter number of hours during which data were collected. Count all young adults who enter the library for any reason.

A. Morning Visits. Morning is from 10 A.M. to noon, or 2 hours.

////

Total morning visits 4

B. Early Afternoon Visits. Early afternoon is from noon to 3 P.M., or 3 hours.

~~////~~ ///

Total early afternoon visits 7

C. After-School Visits. "After School" is from 3 to 6, or 3 hours.

~~////~~ ~~////~~ ~~////~~ ~~////~~ ~~////~~ ~~////~~ ///

Total after-school visits 33

D. Evening Visits. Evening is from 6 to 9 (closing time) or 3 hours.

~~////~~ ~~////~~ ~~////~~ ~~////~~ ~~////~~ /

Total evening visits 26

TOTAL VISITS THIS DAY 70

Figure 2. Worked Example of Form 8: Young Adult Library Visits Tally Sheet

1. Total of all weekday morning visits made during the sample periods. (See Form 8, Section A.) (1) 11

2. Number of weekday morning hours in the sample periods (e.g., 3 hours Monday morning + 3 hours Wednesday morning = 6). (2) 4

3. (1) divided by (2) = average number of weekday morning library visits per hour. (3) 2.75

4. Number of weekday morning hours the library is open each week. (4) 10

5. (4) × (3) = the estimated number of weekday morning visits per week. (5) 27.5=28

6. Repeat steps 1–5 for (a) early afternoon, (b) after school, (c) evening, (d) Saturday, and (e) Sunday hours, and record the estimated number of (6a) weekday early afternoon, (6b) weekday after school, (6c) weekday evening, (6d) Saturday, and (6e) Sunday visits per week.
   (6a) 30
   (6b) 92
   (6c) 75
   (6d) 24
   (6e) 17

7. (5) + (6a) + (6b) + (6c) + (6d) + (6e) = the estimated number of young adult library visits each week. (7) 266

8. Multiply (7) by 12 if this is a summer sample week. This is the estimated Summer Y.A. Library Visits count. If Summer Y.A. Library Visits count was taken earlier, record it in (8). (8) 1,420

9. Multiply (7) by 40 if this is a school year sample week. This is the estimated School Year Y.A. Library Visits count. If School Year Y.A. Library Visits count was taken earlier, record it in (9). (9) 10,640

10. Add (8) and (9) to get the estimated ANNUAL NUMBER OF LIBRARY VISITS BY YOUNG ADULTS. (10) 12,060

11. Record YOUNG ADULT POPULATION OF LEGAL SERVICE AREA. (11) 5,870

12. Divide (10) by (11) to get **Young Adult Library Visits per Young Adult.** (12) 2

Figure 3. Worked Example of Form 7: Young Adult Library Visits Sampling Work Sheet

- Evaluate the environment immediately around the library. Is it a safe place for all young adults to come? (You may need to work with community leaders and decision makers outside the library to solve this problem.)

Further Possibilities

1. For a more detailed picture of library use by young adults relative to the community as a whole, you may also calculate the **Young Adult Library Visits per Capita** by dividing the ANNUAL NUMBER OF LIBRARY VISITS BY YOUNG ADULTS by the *total* POPULATION OF LEGAL SERVICE AREA.
2. Calculate the percentage of total visits to the library made by young adults by dividing the ANNUAL NUMBER OF LIBRARY VISITS BY YOUNG ADULTS by the general ANNUAL NUMBER OF LIBRARY VISITS. This calculation will provide the **Young Adult Library Visits per Total Library Visits** measure. It is then possible to make interesting comparisons, such as: "Young adults make up only 14 percent of the total population of our community, but they account for 37 percent of our total library visits."
3. Look at library visits by young adults during particular time periods, such as the after-school hours from 3:00 to 5:00.
4. Look at **Building Use by Young Adults** in relation to **Young Adult Library Visits per Young Adult.**
5. Relate **Young Adult Library Visits per Young Adult** to Materials Use measures to find out if teenagers are using library materials when they come to the library.

Building Use by Young Adults

Definition:	Average number of young adults in any part of the library at any one time during the year.
Calculation:	Calculate averages from tallies of numbers of young adults in the library at representative times during the day.
Data Collection:	At selected sample times during a typical week in summer and a typical week during the school year, count the number of young adults in all parts of the library.
Example:	During a typical week in summer, staff counted all young adults who were in the library building at the beginning of each of the 55 hours that the library was open. The total number of young adults counted was 235. They divided this total by 55 to find the average, the Summer Building Use by Young Adults (4.3). In a typical week during the school year, they again counted young adults in the library at the beginning of each of the 55 open hours. The total number of young adults counted was 462. They divided 462 by 55 to find the School Year Building Use by Young Adults (8.4). To calculate the annual **Building Use by Young Adults,** it was necessary to weight the two averages to account for the length of the school year, which is three times longer than summer. They multiplied the School Year Building Use by Young Adults (8.4) by 3; the result is 25.2. Add 25.2 and 4.3 (the Summer Building Use by Young Adults) for a total of 29.5. Divide 29.5 by 4 to calculate the annual **Building Use by Young Adults**; the result is 7.4. On average, there are 7.4 young adults in the library at any particular time during the year.

$$\frac{235}{55} = 4.3 \qquad \frac{462}{55} = 8.4 \qquad \frac{4.3 + (8.4 \times 3)}{4} = 7.4$$

Collecting the Data

1. Decide on the typical week in summer and the typical week during the school year in which you want to take the measure. **Building Use by Young Adults** may vary considerably between the summer and the school months.
2. Divide the library into convenient, identifiable areas or spaces for counting purposes. Looking

at a map or floor plan may help if your library is quite large or complex. Some possibilities include the young adult area, homework center, the children's reading room, the children's stacks, adult reference room, adult reading room, adult stacks, periodicals area, audiovisual area, and circulation desk. Be sure that you account for all spaces in the library. Write these areas in the "Spaces" column of the Building Use by Young Adults Data Collection Form (Form 9). You may need to use two pages of the form to account for all spaces.

3. Determine the times during the day when you will be taking the count. You may want hour-by-hour totals. Be sure that the data collection periods are representative of all hours that the building is in use, that is, mornings, early afternoon, late afternoon, and evening. Write the times that the tally will be taken in the spaces marked "Time" on Form 9, Building Use by Young Adults Data Collection Form.
4. At the designated times, a staff person or volunteer walks through the library and counts all young adults in each of the spaces listed on the form. (You may need to provide guidance to the data collector on how to identify a young adult.) Enter the number of young adult users in the appropriate cells on Form 9, Building Use by Young Adults Data Collection Form. Figure 4 is an example of a completed Building Use by Young Adults Data Collection Form.

Calculating the Measure

1. Add the total number of young adults who were counted at all observation times.
2. Divide the total number of young adults by the total number of observation times to find the average Building Use by Young Adults for the sample period.
3. To find an annual **Building Use by Young Adults,** collect data during a typical summer week and a typical week during the school year. Calculate Summer Building Use by Young Adults and School Year Building Use by Young Adults as described in steps 1 and 2.
4. Because the school year is three times longer than the summer, the School Year Building Use by Young Adults needs to be weighted three times as heavily as the Summer Building Use in calculating an annual rate. To do this, multiply the School Year Building Use by Young Adults by 3 to get the weighted School Year Building Use by Young Adults.
5. Add the weighted School Year Building Use by Young Adults and the Summer Building Use by Young Adults and divide by 4 to calculate the **Building Use by Young Adults**.

Interpreting and Using the Data

1. Remember that the **Building Use by Young Adults** figure, like the other output measures is an annual measure. It should be recalculated yearly to see trends in building use.
2. The **Building Use by Young Adults** measure helps to represent the intensity of library use by teenagers. A smaller building may tend to yield smaller numbers for this measure than a large facility.
3. Analyze the **Building Use by Young Adults** at different times of the day or at different times of the year. The results may suggest necessary shifts in staffing. See if **Building Use by Young Adults** increases as a result of a publicity campaign or after-school visits by the young adult librarian or when there are young adult programs scheduled.

Further Possibilities

1. Look at use of subsets of the building, such as **Reference Room Use by Young Adults** or **Mezzanine Lounge Use by Young Adults.**
2. Calculate a **Building Use by Young Adults** for a particular time period, such as **Saturday Building Use by Young Adults** or **After-School Building Use by Young Adults.**

1 of 6

Library Memorial Date Mon., Oct. 21

At sampling time, go quickly through the library and count the number of young adults in each of the following spaces.

Spaces	Users										
	Time: 11AM	Time: 1PM	Time: 3PM	Time: 5PM	Time: 7PM	Time: 8:30	Time:	Time:	Time:	Time:	Time:
YA area	0	0	3	2	4	1					
Children's room	0	0	1	1	2	1					
Adult reference	0	1	4	2	3	2					
Adult reading room	1	0	8	6	10	11					
Circulation desk	0	0	2	3	2	2					
AV section	1	0	4	2	2	2					
Total	2	1	22	16	23	19					

Figure 4. Worked Example of Form 9: Building Use by Young Adults Data Collection Form

Furniture/Equipment Use by Young Adults

Definition:	The proportion of time, on average, that a particular type of furniture or equipment anywhere in the library is being used by a young adult. The specific measure will designate the particular piece of furniture or equipment whose use is being measured; i.e., Computer Use by Young Adults.
Calculation:	Divide the number of items of furniture or equipment in question that are in use by young adults by the number of items available.
Data Collection:	Count total number of items of the particular furniture or equipment in question. Tally the number of each type of item in use by young adults at designated time periods. Tallies are taken during two sample periods during the year, one week in summer and one during the school year, and are generalized for an annual **Furniture/Equipment Use by Young Adults.**
Example:	There are 3 public access computers in the library. The library is open 35 hours a week. During a typical week in summer, staff counted young adults who were using the computers at the beginning of each of the 35 open hours and calculated the use rate for each of the 35 observations by dividing the young adult users at each time by the number of available computers. To calculate the Summer Computer Use by Young Adults, total the 35 individual use rates and divide by 35. The result for this library was .25, or 25 percent. During a typical week during the school year, staff repeated the same data collection and calculation procedures. The School Year Computer Use by Young Adults was .32 or 32 percent. To calculate the annual **Computer Use by Young Adults,** multiply the School Year Computer Use by 3 (to get .96) and add the Summer Computer Use (.25) for a total of 1.21. Divide by 4 to get the final figure. The result in this case is .3, or 30 percent. A computer in the library is used by a young adult 30 percent of the time.

$$.32 \times 3 = .96 \qquad .96 + .25 = 1.21 \qquad \frac{1.21}{4} = .30$$

Collecting the Data

1. Note that the use rate of any furniture or equipment can be calculated. The example is a calculation of the use rate by young adults of public access computers. Other furniture or equipment that may be of interest include online catalog terminals, copy machines, seating of various types, homework centers, and study carrels.
2. Decide on the sample week during the school year and during the summer in which you want to take this measure.
3. Decide which furniture or equipment use to measure. It is not necessary to calculate use rates for all furniture and equipment; do it only for those items that are accessible to young adult users and are of interest to you. List the furniture and equipment whose use is to be measured on Form 10, Furniture/Equipment Use by Young Adults Data Collection Form.
4. Count the total number of each piece of furniture or equipment in question that is available. Record in the "Number Available" column on the Furniture/Equipment Use by Young Adults Data Collection Form.
5. Decide the times at which the tally will be taken and record these in the "Time" spaces on the form. Be sure that you include times that are representative of all hours that the library is open, including mornings, afternoons, evenings, and weekends.
6. At the sampling times, a staff member or volunteer walks through the library and counts the number of each piece of designated furniture or equipment being used by young adults. For this measure, count furniture or equipment, not users. If two young adults are using a single piece of equipment, count as a single use. Figure 5 is an example of a completed Furniture/Equipment Use by Young Adults Data Collection Form.

___ of ___

Location or Department ______________________ Date __________

At sampling time, go quickly through the library and count the number of young adults using each of the following.

(Use Rate is Number in Use by young adults divided by Number Available.)

Furniture/Equipment	Number Available	OBSERVATIONS											
		Time:		Time:		Time:		Time:		Time:		Time:	
		# in Use	Use Rate	# in Use	Use Rate	# in Use	Use Rate	# in Use	Use Rate	# in Use	Use Rate	# in Use	Use Rate
CD-Rom	1	0	0	1	1.00	1	1.00	0	0	0	0	1	1.00
Magazine Index	1	0	0	0	0	1	1.00	1	1.00	1	1.00	0	0
Macs	4	0	0	0	0	3	.75	3	.75	4	1.00	2	.50

Figure 5. Worked Example of Form 10: Furniture/Equipment Use by Young Adults Data Collection Form

7. The person doing the counting may need guidance in identifying young adults.

Calculating the Measure

1. Divide the number of items of furniture or equipment in use by the total number available to get the furniture/equipment use rate by young adults for each observation.
2. To calculate the average Furniture/Equipment Use by Young Adults, total the number of individual use rates *for each separate item of furniture or equipment being counted* from all copies of the Furniture/Equipment Use by Young Adult Data Collection Form and divide by the number of total Use Rates calculated. Note that you will have a separate total figure for each piece of furniture or equipment being counted. For example, in Figure 5, you will calculate an aggregate CD-ROM Use figure, Magazine Index Use figure, and a Mac Use figure. If this is a summer week, these will be Summer Furniture/Equipment Use by Young Adults calculations. The school year calculation is the School Year Furniture/Equipment Use by Young Adults.
3. For an annual **Furniture/Equipment Use by Young Adults** measure, you need to know both the summer and school year calculations of the measure. Weight the School Year Furniture/Equipment Use by Young Adults by multiplying it by 3. Add the weighted School Year Furniture/Equipment Use by Young Adults to the Summer Furniture/Equipment Use by Young Adults and divide the total by 4. The result is the annual **Furniture/ Equipment by Young Adults** measure.

Interpreting and Using the Data

1. Furniture/Equipment Use Rates indicate the likelihood that the piece of furniture or equipment being measured will be in use by a young adult. If all of the items are being used at a given time, the Use Rate for that observation is 1.0 or 100 percent. If half are in use, the Use Rate for that observation is .5 or 50 percent.
2. A high Use Rate indicates that a particular item is well used by young adults. Consistently high Use Rates may mean that a library needs to increase its number of the item in question. It may be necessary to add more computers or copy machines, for example.
3. Low **Furniture/Equipment Use by Young Adults** figures do not necessarily mean that the library is not well used, just that that particular item of furniture or equipment is not used as much by young adults. For example, an affluent community with a high education level may find that the **Computer Use by Young Adults** is quite low because most teenagers have access to a computer at home. Libraries with very high circulation sometimes find that Seating Use Rates are very low because people come in to check out material and leave right away.
4. Some libraries have found that the Furniture/Equipment Use Rates are useful when planning for new equipment or doing building expansion space planning.

Further Possibilities

1. Calculate general **Furniture/Equipment Use Rates** by all users. Compare the results with **Furniture/Equipment Use by Young Adults.**
2. Calculate **Furniture/Equipment Use by Young Adults** for particular times of the day to document when usage is most intense.

Homework Center Visits per Young Adult

Definition:	Number of young adults using the homework center during the year relative to the number of young adults in the community.
Calculation:	ANNUAL NUMBER OF HOMEWORK CENTER VISITS BY YOUNG ADULTS divided by YOUNG ADULT POPULATION OF LEGAL SERVICE AREA.
Data Collection:	Count young adults using the homework center during one week in summer and one week during the school year.
Example:	During one sample week in summer, 15 young adults used the homework center. Multiply 15 by 12 to find Summer Homework Center Visits; the result is 180. During one sample week during the school year, 35 young adults used the homework center. Multiply 35 by 40 to find School Year Homework Visits; the result is 1,400. Add the Summer Homework Center Visits (180) to the School Year Homework Center Visits (1,400) to find the ANNUAL NUMBER OF HOMEWORK CENTER VISITS BY YOUNG ADULTS; the result is 1,580. There are 2,000 young adults living in this community. Divide the ANNUAL NUMBER OF HOMEWORK CENTER VISITS BY YOUNG ADULTS (1,580) by the YOUNG ADULT POPULATION OF LEGAL SERVICE AREA (2,000) to find the **Homework Center Visits per Young Adult** measure. The result is .79. On average, 79 percent of the young adults in the community used the homework center during the year.

$$\frac{(15 \times 12) + (35 \times 40)}{2{,}000} = .79$$

Collecting the Data

1. A homework center may be an elaborately equipped special room in the library or just a table in a corner with a computer and some special reference tools and study aids. Its purpose is to help students find and use materials for their homework assignments. Some libraries restrict homework center usage to people of school age; others make it available to anyone who wants to use its resources. For this output measure, you will count only young adults using the homework center.
2. Select a typical week in summer and a typical week during the school year to collect the data. It is important to count in summer as well as during the school year even if students in your area do not attend school in the summer. Most homework centers are at least occasionally used for purposes other than homework.
3. Decide whether you want to count all young adults using the homework center during all periods of the week or whether, because of staffing constraints, you need to sample "typical" hours during the sample week. See the discussion of sampling in Part 2 for guidance in arranging a sampling schedule. Use Form 11, Homework Center Visits Sampling Work Sheet, to calculate your results if you are using the sampling option.
4. During all scheduled data collection hours, have someone, staff or volunteer, count all young adults who use the homework center. The counter should be vigilant and rigorous about counting all young adult users but should avoid making people at the homework center feel that they are under surveillance. Prominent signs announcing that you are taking this count will help to explain the data collector's behavior.
5. Use Form 12, Homework Center Visits Tally Sheet, to count the young adult homework center users. You may design a more detailed form if you are interested in having an hourly count. Calculation of the output measure requires only the daily count if you are counting during all open hours.

Calculating the Measure

1. At the end of the sample week, enter your data on the Homework Center Visits Sampling Work Sheet if you collected data during

selected hours. If you counted users during all open hours, just add up all visits.

2. If this is a summer week, multiply your total by 12 to find the Summer Homework Center Visits by Young Adults. If this is a school year week, multiply your total by 40 to find the School Year Homework Center Visits by Young Adults.
3. Add the Summer Homework Center Visits by Young Adults total and the School Year Homework Center Visits by Young Adults total to find the ANNUAL NUMBER OF HOMEWORK CENTER VISITS BY YOUNG ADULTS. Divide the ANNUAL NUMBER OF HOMEWORK CENTER VISITS BY YOUNG ADULTS by the YOUNG ADULT POPULATION OF LEGAL SERVICE AREA to find the **Homework Center Visits per Young Adult.**

Interpreting and Using the Data

1. Unless your homework center is unusually well-used, the **Homework Center Visits per Young Adult** measure will probably be less than 1.0. It will indicate the percentage of the young adult population, on average, that uses the homework center during the year.
2. The measure does not indicate the number of different individuals who use the homework center, only the average proportion of the population that does. The 20/80 rule would suggest that the same 20 young adults may be responsible for 80 percent of the usage. Your own informed observations will tell you how applicable this rule of thumb might be in your own situation. Your measure is still statistically accurate; you just want to be cautious about how you represent the measure or apply it to practice.
3. This measure is obviously a significant one for libraries with a major stake in the Support to Formal Education role. It also can be used to demonstrate a library's commitment to positive after-school programming for youth.

Further Possibilities

1. Use the **Furniture/Equipment Use by Young Adults** data collection method to calculate a **Homework Center Visits by Young Adults.** It will indicate the intensity of use of the Homework Center by teenagers.
2. If you are just about to open a homework center, take the **Young Adult Homework Fill Rate** measure before and six months after the homework center is opened to see if it has made a difference in the fill rate.
3. Compare usage of the homework center by young adults and by other age groups.

Materials Use Measures

Materials Use measures are indicators of the extent to which the materials collection is used. Six different approaches to measuring materials use are offered here. While all are derived from *Output Measures for Public Libraries,* second edition, some involve differences in data collection techniques because of the need to make a physical link between the young adult library patrons and the material that they are using.

Circulation of Young Adult Materials per Young Adult measures the annual use of materials labeled as young adult that are loaned for use outside the library, relative to the number of young adults in the community.

Circulation of Materials per Young Adult measures the annual use of all library materials from any section of the library that are loaned for use outside the library to young adults relative to the number of young adults in the community.

In-Library Use of Young Adult Materials per Young Adult indicates the annual use of young adult materials within the library relative to the number of young adults in the community served.

In-Library Use of Materials by Young Adults per Young Adult measures the annual use of materials from all parts of the collection by young adults within the library relative to the number of young adults in the community served.

Turnover Rate of Young Adult Materials measures the annual circulation of young adult materials relative to the total size of the young adult collection. It indicates the intensity of use of the young adult collection.

Circulation of Young Adult Materials per Young Adult

Definition: The average annual circulation of young adult materials per young adult in the community served.

Calculation: ANNUAL CIRCULATION OF YOUNG ADULT MATERIALS divided by YOUNG ADULT POPULATION OF LEGAL SERVICE AREA.

Data Collection: Collected by the automated circulation system or by a tally taken at the circulation desk during a typical week in summer and a typical week during the school year.

Example: A library with a YOUNG ADULT POPULATION of LEGAL SERVICE AREA of 350 had an ANNUAL CIRCULATION OF YOUNG ADULT MATERIALS of 1,200. The **Circulation of Young Adult Materials per Young Adult** is 3.43. On average, each young adult in the community checked out three items from the young adult collection during the year.

$$\frac{1{,}200}{350} = 3.43$$

Collecting the Data

1. The ANNUAL CIRCULATION OF YOUNG ADULT MATERIALS is the total circulation to all users of all materials in all formats that are labeled young adult. It includes books, magazines, compact discs, etc. It does not distinguish between young adults and other users. It requires that young adult materials be marked in such a way that the automated circulation system can track them or that circulation staff can easily identify them.

2. The easiest and most reliable way to establish the ANNUAL CIRCULATION OF YOUNG ADULT MATERIALS is to collect it from the records of the automated circulation system. Be sure that you know exactly which materials your automated circulation system counts as young adult. Sometimes only young adult books are counted, with young adult audiovisual materials going into a general count of all audiovisual materials circulated. Some automated systems require you to take several different figures and total them to get an annual count of all young adult materials. Be sure you have found all the appropriate data. If your system does not presently track the circulation of all young adult materials, you may want to investigate adding this data element.

3. If your circulation system does not record young adult materials that are checked out, you will have to tally this figure by hand. You can do this with a simple hand tally or clicker at the circulation desk.

4. Some libraries may want to make the tabulation of young adult circulation a routine that is done every time a young adult item is checked out during the year. Most will prefer to do this during two sample weeks, a typical week in summer and a typical week during the school year.

5. Instruct circulation staff to make a hash mark or click the tabulator every time they check out a book, magazine, cassette tape, compact disc, or video that is labeled young adult. During the sample weeks, you should observe the circulation desk closely to be sure that this practice is being followed consistently. Remind each new shift at the desk about the young adult circulation tally. Have a prominent sign at the checkout machine.
6. Keep your tally at all times during the week that books are checked out. Do not attempt to sample hours during the week for this count.
7. Count young adult items being renewed as circulations. Count young adult books on interlibrary loan from other agencies as well. Do not count young adult books that you are lending to another library, however. They will be counted as items circulated at the agency that receives them when they are checked out to the patron.

Calculating the Measure

1. If you have the data from your automated circulation system, divide the ANNUAL CIRCULATION OF YOUNG ADULT MATERIALS by the YOUNG ADULT POPULATION OF LEGAL SERVICE AREA.
2. If you have collected the data from a hand tally, take the total from the summer week and multiply by 12 for the Summer Circulation of Young Adult Materials. Take the total from the school year week and multiply by 40 for the School Year Circulation of Young Adult Materials. Add the Summer Circulation of Young Adult Materials and the School Year Circulation of Young Adult Materials to find the ANNUAL CIRCULATION OF YOUNG ADULT MATERIALS. Divide the ANNUAL CIRCULATION OF YOUNG ADULT MATERIALS by the YOUNG ADULT POPULATION OF LEGAL SERVICE AREA to find the **Circulation of Young Adult Materials per Young Adult.**

Interpreting and Using the Data

1. The **Circulation of Young Adult Materials per Young Adult** figure represents only the average usage of young adult materials. Keep in mind that most young adults use many parts of the collection when you are characterizing overall young adult usage.
2. A low **Circulation of Young Adult Materials per Young Adult** could be balanced by a high **In-Library Use of Young Adult Materials per Young Adult.** Maybe young adults don't check out materials but read them in the library.
3. Libraries that have adopted the role Popular Materials Library will probably aim for a relatively high **Circulation of Young Adult Materials per Young Adult.** Roles such as Community Activity Services, Community Information Services, Research Center, and Independent Learning Center place less emphasis on circulation of materials.
4. This output measure can be helpful in evaluating the young adult collection itself. If you want to increase this measure:
   - Consider changing the focus of the young adult collection. Add more paperbacks. Buy multiple copies of popular titles. Buy multiple copies of popular magazines.
   - Consider changing the organization of the young adult collection. If it is currently arranged in traditional library order with the fiction alphabetical by author and the nonfiction by Dewey, consider arranging it by broad reader interests instead.
   - Highlight very popular materials. Some libraries devote entire racks to paperback books by single popular young adult authors. Make the popular series books very easy to find.
   - Look at the **Young Adult Fill Rates** or do a quick user survey to find out how satisfied young adults are with the materials in the young adult collection.

Further Possibilities

1. Add ANNUAL IN-LIBRARY USE OF YOUNG ADULT MATERIALS to ANNUAL CIRCULATION OF YOUNG ADULT MATERIALS to find the total USE OF YOUNG ADULT MATERIALS. Divide by the YOUNG ADULT POPULATION OF LEGAL SERVICE AREA to find the **Use of Young Adult Materials per Young Adult.**
2. Collect separate data on circulation of particular formats of young adult material that interest you. Calculate **Circulation of Young Adult Books per Young Adult** or **Circulation of Young Adult Audio Materials per Young Adult,** for example.

Circulation of Materials per Young Adult

Definition:	The annual circulation of all library materials to young adults relative to the number of young adults in the community served
Calculation:	ANNUAL CIRCULATION OF LIBRARY MATERIALS TO YOUNG ADULTS divided by YOUNG ADULT POPULATION OF LEGAL SERVICE AREA.
Data Collection:	Recorded by the automated circulation system, taken by a hand tally, or counted from Form 15, Young Adult Library Survey, used primarily for collecting data for **Young Adult Fill Rate**.
Example:	Circulation staff tallied 200 items checked out by young adult patrons during a typical week in summer. Multiply 200 by 12 to find the Summer Young Adult Circulation; the figure is 2,400. They tallied 430 items checked out by young adults during a typical week during the school year. Multiply 430 by 40 to find the School Year Young Adult Circulation; the figure is 17,200. Add the Summer Young Adult Circulation (2,400) and the School Year Young Adult Circulation (17,200) to find the ANNUAL CIRCULATION OF LIBRARY MATERIALS TO YOUNG ADULTS; the figure is 19,600. The YOUNG ADULT POPULATION OF LEGAL SERVICE AREA is 980. Divide the ANNUAL CIRCULATION OF LIBRARY MATERIALS TO YOUNG ADULTS by the YOUNG ADULT POPULATION OF LEGAL SERVICE AREA to find the **Circulation of Materials per Young Adult**; the figure is 20. On average, each young adult in the community checked out 20 books during the year.

$$\frac{(12 \times 200) + (40 \times 740)}{980} = 20$$

Collecting the Data

1. The easiest way to collect the circulation data is from an automated circulation system that has the capability of counting materials checked out by young adults. (In practice, this usually means materials checked out with young adult library cards.) If your circulation system cannot provide data about circulation of materials by young adults, following are two alternative methods for collecting it.

Alternative 1

1. During a typical summer week and a typical week during the school year, have circulation staff make a hash mark or click a tabulator for every item in every format from every part of the collection that is checked out on a young adult library card.
2. If you do not issue special cards to young adult borrowers, the circulation staff must identify by sight all young adult borrowers. This identification can be facilitated by having prominent signage at the circulation desk that says: "We are counting young adult circulation this week. Please let us know if you are between the ages of 12 and 18 when you check out your materials. Thank you for your help."
3. During your sample weeks, give special attention to circulation procedures. Be sure that staff remember to take the tally. Remind staff as each shift changes that you are counting circulation by young adults this week.

Alternative 2

1. If you are collecting data for the **Young Adult Fill Rate**, there is a line on the Young Adult Library Survey, Form 15, that asks "How many items (books, magazines, tapes, etc.) did you check out today?" (Form 15A is a Spanish translation of the form.) If you retrieve a Young Adult Library Survey from every young adult patron during your two data collection weeks, you can total these for an indicator of young adult circulation.
2. Do not use these data as the basis for the ANNUAL CIRCULATION OF LIBRARY MATERIALS TO YOUNG ADULTS if you sample hours during your typical week. You will get incomplete figures from which it is not possible to generalize to an annual statistic.

3. This method is the least reliable for collecting the ANNUAL CIRCULATION OF LIBRARY MATERIALS TO YOUNG ADULTS. It will probably result in an undercount of the actual circulation because you will miss some young adult patrons and because it relies on their accurately reporting circulation on the form.

Calculating the Measure

1. If you have an ANNUAL CIRCULATION OF LIBRARY MATERIALS TO YOUNG ADULTS figure from your automated system, simply divide it by the YOUNG ADULT POPULATION OF LEGAL SERVICE AREA.
2. If you have used either of the two alternative data collection methods, add all tallies from the circulation desk or all circulation figures from Form 15, Young Adult Library Survey. Multiply the total from the summer week by 12 to find the Summer Circulation of Materials to Young Adults. Multiply the total from the school year week by 40 to find the School Year Circulation of Materials to Young Adults. Add the Summer Circulation of Materials to Young Adults and the School Year Circulation of Materials to Young Adults to find the ANNUAL CIRCULATION OF LIBRARY MATERIALS TO YOUNG ADULTS. Divide by the YOUNG ADULT POPULATION OF LEGAL SERVICE AREA to find the **Circulation of Materials per Young Adult.**

Interpreting and Using the Data

1. Because of some of the difficulties inherent in data collection for this measure, it is somewhat less reliable than many other output measures. However, if you are consistent in your data collection, it will give you information that you can compare over time.
2. Compare the **Circulation of Materials per Young Adult** figure with the **Circulation of Young Adult Materials per Young Adult**. This will give you a sense of the relative uses of the young adult collection and the general collection by young adults. Keep in mind that young adult materials are included in this overall library materials circulation count.
3. Compare the **Circulation of Materials per Young Adult** figure with the overall **Circulation per Capita** to see how young adult usage of the collection compares with overall circulation. Compare it with adult and children's circulation if those figures are available and comparable, that is, based on circulation of all materials on adult or children's library cards.

In-Library Use of Young Adult Materials per Young Adult

Definition:	Number of young adult materials used in the library during a given year per young adult in the community served.
Calculation:	ANNUAL IN-LIBRARY USE OF YOUNG ADULT MATERIALS divided by YOUNG ADULT POPULATION OF LEGAL SERVICE AREA.
Data Collection:	For two typical weeks during the year, ask users not to reshelve any materials. Count all young adult materials.
Example:	During a typical week in summer, staff counted 100 young adult material items that were left unshelved by patrons. Multiply 100 by 12 to find the Summer In-Library Use of Young Adult Materials; the figure is 1,200. For a typical week during the school year, staff counted 200 young adult materials left unshelved. Multiply 200 by 40 to find the School Year In-Library Use of Young Adult Materials; the figure is 8,000. Add the Summer In-Library Use of Young Adult Materials (1,200) and the School Year In-Library Use of Young Adult Materials (8,000) to find the ANNUAL IN-LIBRARY USE OF YOUNG ADULT MATERIALS (9,200). Divide the ANNUAL IN-LIBRARY USE OF YOUNG ADULT MATERIALS (9,200) by the YOUNG ADULT POPULATION OF LEGAL SERVICE AREA (2,000 in this case). The **In-Library Use of Young Adult Materials per Young Adult** is 4.6. On average, each young adult in the community used 4.6 young adult materials in the library during the year.

$$\frac{(100 \times 12) + (200 \times 40)}{2{,}000} = 4.6$$

Collecting the Data

1. Collect data during one typical summer week and one typical week during the school year.
2. Make a special effort to ask users not to reshelve materials during this week. Have signs posted everywhere throughout the library: "Survey in progress. Please do not reshelve materials."

   Make it easy for people to follow these directions. Place boxes or baskets or book trucks throughout the library with big signs on them, "Please do not reshelve your materials; put them here." Or put signs on the tables: "Please do not reshelve your materials. Leave them here."
3. Do not make a special effort to target young adults. Ask *all* patrons to leave their materials unshelved. It will be relatively easy to calculate in-library use rates for adult and children's materials as well as young adult materials if you wish.
4. Data collection for this output measure requires that all young adult materials be labeled as such.
5. At designated times during the day, collect and count all young adult materials left on tables, on the floor, on tops of counters, and at your collection points, such as boxes and baskets. It doesn't matter how many times you take the count as long as you reshelve the materials you count each time so the items are not counted again. (They need not be reshelved on the regular shelves; they may be placed on sorting shelves.) If library staff members have a regular daily schedule for clearing off tables, the count could be taken at those times. Be sure that the staff does not clear tables without taking a count.
6. Be sure that your data collectors know to count young adult materials in all formats, including magazines and audiovisual materials. The list of kinds of material on Form 13 should help remind them. Feel free to add other categories to meet your own needs. If you do not need to know this level of detail, ignore the categories and record only the totals at the bottom.
7. Record the counts on Form 13, In-Library Use of Young Adult Materials Log. Use one form for each day of the week. Figure 6 is an example of a completed In-Library Use of Young Adult Materials Log.

Calculating the Measure

1. Add up the totals from each day's In-Library Use of Young Adult Materials Log for a weekly total.
2. If the sample week is in the summer, multiply your total by 12 for the Summer In-Library Use of Young Adult Materials. If the sample week is a school year week, multiply your total by 40 to find the School Year In-Library Use of Young Adult Materials.
3. Add the Summer In-Library Use of Young Adult Materials and the School Year In-Library Use of Young Adult Materials to find the ANNUAL IN-LIBRARY USE OF YOUNG ADULT MATERIALS.
4. Divide the ANNUAL IN-LIBRARY USE OF YOUNG ADULT MATERIALS by the YOUNG ADULT POPULATION OF LEGAL SERVICE AREA to find the **In-Library Use of Young Adult Materials per Young Adult.**

Interpreting and Using the Data

1. A high **In-Library Use of Young Adult Materials per Young Adult** may be associated with a

Date Tues., Feb. 18

Use one tally sheet each day. Enter times at the top of the form. At each time listed on the log, collect and count the young adult materials left for reshelving on tables, tops of shelves, floor, etc.

Type of Material	Time: 11AM	Time: 1PM	Time: 3PM	Time: 5PM	Time: 8 PM	TOTAL
Paperbacks	0	2	8	6	3	19
Hardcover Fiction	0	0	1	2	1	4
Hardcover Nonfiction	0	0	2	4	2	8
Magazines	3	2	6	4	3	18
Cassette Tapes; CDs	0	0	1	2	1	4
Other Cliffnotes	0	0	3	6	1	10
Other	0	0	0	0	0	—
Other	0	0	0	0	0	—
TOTAL	3	4	21	24	11	63

Figure 6. Worked Example of Form 13: In-Library Use of Young Adult Materials Log

high **Young Adult Information Transactions per Young Adult.** It may also indicate a community in which young adults prefer or need to use materials in the library rather than taking them home.

2. If you want to increase **In-Library Use of Young Adult Materials per Young Adult,** you might:

   - Increase seating and study areas for young adults
   - Make the library itself more attractive and inviting to young adults
   - Acquire more appealing or useful young adult materials
   - Make some popular browsing materials for in-library reference use only

3. If you want to decrease **In-Library Use of Young Adult Materials per Young Adult** (presumably converting some of these statistics to circulation statistics), consider:

   - Changing some of your reference materials to circulating copies
   - Acquiring additional circulating copies of heavily used reference materials, such as encyclopedias

Further Possibilities

1. Calculate the in-library use of particular kinds of young adult materials, such as magazines.
2. Analyze the **In-Library Use of Young Adult Materials per Young Adult** by time of day.

In-Library Use of Materials by Young Adults per Young Adult

Definition:	Number of materials from any part of the collection used in the library by young adults per young adult in the community served.
Calculation:	ANNUAL IN-LIBRARY USE OF LIBRARY MATERIALS BY YOUNG ADULTS divided by YOUNG ADULT POPULATION OF LEGAL SERVICE AREA.
Data Collection:	All young adult patrons complete a tally of materials they use in the library each time they visit the library during a typical week in summer and a typical week in the school year.
Example:	All young adults using the library during a typical week in summer reported using a total of 40 books in the library. Multiply 40 by 12 to find the Summer In-Library Use of Materials by Young Adults; the total is 480. All young adults using the library during a typical week during the school year reported using a total of 200 books in the library. Multiply 200 by 40 to find the School Year In-Library Use of Materials; the figure is 8,000. Add the Summer In-Library Use of Materials (480) and the School Year In-Library Use of Materials (8,000) to find the ANNUAL IN-LIBRARY USE OF LIBRARY MATERIALS BY YOUNG ADULTS; the figure is 8,480. Divide the ANNUAL IN-LIBRARY USE OF LIBRARY MATERIALS BY YOUNG ADULTS (8,480) by the YOUNG ADULT POPULATION OF LEGAL SERVICE AREA (650) to find the **In-Library Use of Materials by Young Adults per Young Adult.** The figure is 13.05. On average, each young adult in the community used 13 materials in the library during the year.

$$\frac{(40 \times 12) + (200 \times 40)}{650} = 13.05$$

Collecting the Data

1. Select a typical week in summer and a typical week during the school year in which to collect the data.
2. This measure is designed to count *all* materials from all parts of the collection in all formats used by young adults in the library. It is self-reported because there is no way of knowing the age of the patron who has used a book that is left lying on a table. Direct observation might work, but it is impractical to observe the library behavior of all young adult patrons in the library. It would also make the young adults feel very self-conscious. Self-reporting, while somewhat unreliable, at least gives an indication of young adult in-library use of the collection as a whole.
3. During the sample week, give each young adult entering the library a copy of Form 14, Young Adult In-Library Materials Use Tally Sheet. You may need to customize this form to suit the collection scope of your own library. (Form 14A is a Spanish translation of the form.)
4. If possible, take the time to tell each young adult that you are conducting an important survey of young adult use of the library. Ask for his or her cooperation. Tell the young adults to keep the tally with them as they use the library and to make a hash mark each time they use a different item, such as a book, encyclopedia, magazine, pamphlet, etc. Ask them to turn in the form at the circulation desk or the exit as they leave the library. Have a box handy for the completed forms at the circulation desk or the exit. You should also have somebody there to remind young adults to leave the form as they exit the building. This person should have extra blank forms in case the patron has left the tally form somewhere in the library. If this happens, ask the young adult to take a minute and fill the form in before leaving.
5. The form does not measure use of electronic resources; use the **Furniture/Equipment Use by Young Adults** measure to collect those data.
6. Have signs up at strategic points throughout the library reminding young adult patrons to

fill in the tally. While helping young adults with materials, reference librarians and other public service staff might also discreetly remind the patrons to mark the forms.

Calculating the Measure

1. At the end of the week, count the totals from all Young Adult In-Library Use Tally Sheets that were found in the boxes. Ignore those that were left throughout the library even if they have some marks on them. You have no way of knowing whether these are duplicates or whether they are complete; it is safest to discard them.
2. If the sample week is in the summer, multiply the total from the tallies by 12; this figure is the Summer In-Library Use of Materials by Young Adults. If the sample week is during the school year, multiply the total by 40 to find the School Year In-Library Use of Materials by Young Adults.
3. Add the Summer In-Library Use of Materials by Young Adults and the School Year In-Library Use of Materials by Young Adults to find the ANNUAL IN-LIBRARY USE OF LIBRARY MATERIALS BY YOUNG ADULTS. Divide the ANNUAL IN-LIBRARY USE OF LIBRARY MATERIALS BY YOUNG ADULTS by the YOUNG ADULT POPULATION OF LEGAL SERVICE AREA to find the **In-Library Use of Materials by Young Adults per Young Adult.**

Interpreting and Using the Data

1. This measure is inclusive. Since it includes the in-library use of all materials, it subsumes **In-Library Use of Young Adult Materials per Young Adult.** If you trust the self-reporting of your young adult patrons, you could calculate the **In-Library Use of Young Adult Materials per Young Adult.** from the Young Adult In-Library Use Tally Sheets by counting just the items labeled Young Adult from that form.
2. Because the data for this measure are collected by a very different technique than were data for **In-Library Use of Children's Materials per Child** as directed in *Output Measures for Public Library Service to Children* or **In-Library Materials Use per Capita** as directed in *Output Measures for Public Libraries,* second edition, you cannot compare it to either of them. It will be best used in comparison or in conjunction with statistics such as **Circulation of Materials per Young Adult.** You also can use it to compare in-library use of materials by young adults over time in your own library.
3. It may be helpful to look at this measure in relation to homework center measures

Further Possibilities

1. Calculate in-library use rates for different kinds of materials, such as reference books.
2. Calculate in-library use rates by young adults for different time periods, such as after school or Saturdays.

Turnover Rate of Young Adult Materials

Definition:	The annual circulation of young adult materials per young adult volumes owned.
Calculation:	ANNUAL CIRCULATION OF YOUNG ADULT MATERIALS divided by YOUNG ADULT MATERIALS HOLDINGS.
Data Collection:	Use data collected for **Circulation of Young Adult Materials per Young Adult** and existing data about the size of the young adult collection.
Example:	The YOUNG ADULT MATERIALS HOLDINGS of a library consist of 500 cataloged items and 2,000 uncataloged paperbacks, for a total of 2,500 items. The ANNUAL CIRCULATION OF YOUNG ADULT MATERIALS is 8,000. Divide the ANNUAL CIRCULATION OF YOUNG ADULT MATERIALS (8,000) by the YOUNG ADULT MATERIALS HOLDINGS (2,500) to find the **Turnover Rate of Young Adult Materials.** The figure is 3.2. On average, each item in the young adult materials collection circulated 3.2 times during the past year. $\frac{8{,}000}{2{,}500} = 3.2$

Collecting the Data and Calculating the Measure

1. The ANNUAL CIRCULATION OF YOUNG ADULT MATERIALS is the total circulation of all materials labeled young adult to all patrons. See the output measure **Circulation of Young Adult Materials per Young Adult** for details about how to collect these data.
2. The YOUNG ADULT MATERIALS HOLDINGS are the total number of cataloged and uncataloged materials that are labeled young adult. Do not count periodicals, whether cataloged or not. The figure should include *all* copies of *all* titles.
3. If you do not already have the data for YOUNG ADULT MATERIALS HOLDINGS, see *Output Measures for Public Libraries,* second edition, and *Output Measures for Public Library Service to Children* for some suggestions about how to estimate your holdings from shelf list data. This estimation can be difficult now that more and more libraries are abandoning their shelf lists; try to get the figure from existing data. See if your automated circulation system can generate the data if you do not have the information already.
4. To calculate the **Turnover Rate of Young Adult Materials,** simply divide the ANNUAL CIRCULATION OF YOUNG ADULT MATERIALS by the YOUNG ADULT MATERIALS HOLDINGS.

Interpreting the Data

1. Turnover in this measure indicates the average number of times during the year that each item in the young adult collection circulates.
2. Most young adult collections emphasize high-interest, popular materials; therefore, they should have high turnover rates relative to the total collection. Larger, more-general collections will tend to have lower turnover rates.
3. A high **Turnover Rate of Young Adult Materials** may result in a low **Young Adult Fill Rate.** Young adults may find that the specific items they are looking for are always checked out.
4. If you want to increase the **Turnover Rate of Young Adult Materials,** think about these ideas:
   - Weed the collection often. Take out "shelf-sitters" and books in dilapidated condition.
   - Buy multiple copies of popular materials.
   - Use merchandising techniques to focus attention on your materials.
   - Keep the collection lean, current, and popular.
   - Look at the suggestions for increasing **Circulation of Young Adult Materials per Young Adult.**
   - Be sure that your holdings figure reflects all withdrawals. It is easy to lose track of holdings, particularly when the collection is primarily a browsing collection of uncataloged paperbacks. Be sure to add new purchases to the figure too, of course.

Further Possibilities

1. Compute turnover rates for specific types of materials. To do this calculation, you will need to be able to determine both circulation and holdings for each type of item.
2. Calculate an **In-Library Turnover Rate of Young Adult Materials** by dividing the ANNUAL IN-LIBRARY USE OF YOUNG ADULT MATERIALS by YOUNG ADULT MATERIALS HOLDINGS.
3. It is neither practical nor particularly useful to calculate a turnover rate that reflects young adult use of the entire collection. It may be possible, however, to look at young adult turnover rates for segments of the collection, such as videos or compact discs.

Materials Availability Measures

The materials availability measures are variants of the fill rates presented in *Output Measures for Public Libraries,* second edition. They indicate the degree to which young adult patrons are able to find the materials they are looking for when they come to the library. The measures are expressed as the percentage of searches for particular items that are successful.

The data for calculating the fill rates are taken from user surveys. The survey form in this book has been tested with many young adults, and it works very well. Teenagers seem agreeable to filling it out, even eager in some cases. In field tests, there were only a few cases of obvious scams, when groups of young adults suddenly found great amusement in filling in the form with "made up" information.

Young Adult Fill Rate

Definition:	The percentage of successful searches by young adults for library materials in any part of the library collection.
Calculation:	Number of successful searches divided by all searches.
Data Collection:	A survey of young adult library users taken during two sample periods, one in summer and one during the school year.
Example:	During the summer sample period, one library counted 102 items sought by the young adults who filled out the library survey forms. The library counted 89 items found, for a Summer Young Adult Fill Rate of 87 percent (89 divided by 102). During the school year sample period, the library counted 200 items sought, and a total of 142 found. The School Year Young Adult Fill Rate is 71 percent (142 divided by 200). To find the annual **Young Adult Fill Rate,** convert the percentages to decimals. Multiply the School Year Young Adult Fill Rate by 3; the figure is 2.13. Add the Summer Young Adult Fill Rate to the weighted School Year Fill Rate; the figure is 3.0. Divide by 4. For this library, the **Young Adult Fill Rate** is .75 or 75 percent. On average, there was a 75 percent chance that a young adult's search for a particular item in the library was successful during the past year.

$$\frac{89}{102} = .87 \qquad \frac{142}{200} = .71 \qquad \frac{.87 + (3 \times .71)}{4} = .75$$

Collecting the Data

Scheduling the Survey

1. Select a typical week during the summer and a typical week during the school year to collect your data.
2. You must be able to collect and count at least 100 usable surveys from young adult library patrons during the sample period to make valid assumptions about the data. If you cannot collect 100 surveys in a one-week period, you will need to extend the time to two weeks.
3. Administer the survey during all hours that the library is open, targeting *every* young adult library user during the sample period, if possible. However, if staffing constraints dictate a sampling approach, then be sure that you distribute surveys during representative hours that young adults are in the library. You will distort the results if you survey only after school or if you oversample during the mornings, when most young adults are in school. See the discussion of sampling in Part 2 for more guidance.

Administering the Survey

1. One person should be responsible for the survey. The survey coordinator should train all staff who will be involved in the survey, prepare materials, schedule data collectors, and collect the survey forms.
2. Be sure that *all* staff are aware that the survey is taking place and that they know its purpose. All staff should be able to answer basic questions about the survey from the public and refer appropriate queries to the survey coordinator.
3. Pretesting your procedures is essential; this pretest will help you to identify unforeseen problems.
4. Duplicate enough copies of Form 15, Young Adult Library Survey, to be able to give one to *every* young adult entering the library during the sample period. Form 15A is a Spanish version of the Young Adult Library Survey. Figure 7 is an example of a completed Young Adult Library Survey.
5. Number the forms so you will know how many were given out and how many came back.
6. Post signs indicating that a young adult library survey is being taken. The wording could be something like: "Attention, young adults! We are taking a library survey this week. Please fill out the Young Adult Library Survey forms before you leave today. Thank you!"
7. During the sample period, give a form to all young adult library users, preferably as they

Form # 4

1. How many items (books, magazines, tapes, etc.) did you check out today? 5

2. Were you looking for anything in particular in the library? YES NO

   If you were just browsing, skip down to question 3.

   If you were looking for particular things, please list them here:

   a. Books about American Revolution

   Did you find it? YES NO

   Was it for school? YES NO

   b. Video — Nightmare on Elm St.

   Did you find it? YES NO

   Was it for school? YES NO

   c. Carrie

   Did you find it? YES NO

   Was it for school? YES NO

   (If you were looking for more than three things, please list them on the back.)

3. If you were just browsing and not looking for anything special, did you find anything interesting? YES NO

4. Did you come to the library for some completely different reason, such as attending a program or meeting a friend or using the restroom? YES NO

5. How old are you? 15

6. Is there anything else you want to tell us about the library? You may write on the back of the page if you want to.

Thank you for answering our questions today! Please leave this form in the marked box when you leave the library.

Figure 7. Worked Example of Form 15: Young Adult Library Survey

enter the library. It is not enough to simply have the forms available for the young adults to take. You must make a friendly, nonaggressive personal contact with all young adult users and ask them to fill out the form. The data collector should ask the young adult to leave the completed form in the marked box at the circulation desk or exit on the way out.

8. Survey distributors may need some guidance in identifying young adults. During training, provide information that may assist them, but don't worry about it too much. The age line on the survey will enable you to eliminate any forms from patrons who are too young or too old. If the survey distributor is standing next to the sign that announces a young adult survey in progress, some people may volunteer or offer the information that they are too old or too young.
9. If a young adult refuses to take a form, the survey distributor should mark it "refused" and drop it in the collection box.

Calculating the Data

1. A staff member who is familiar with young adult library materials should do the tabulating. Some responses will require an informed eye to determine what was really meant.
2. Use the Young Adult Library Survey Log (Form 16). You will need enough copies to record all the survey forms that were distributed. Write the number of each form in the first column.
3. In column (1), enter information drawn from the question "Were you looking for anything special in the library?"
4. Column (2) records information about browsing searches.
5. Column (3) is for recording other uses of the library and forms that were blank or refused.
6. Add up each column and enter the totals on the bottom line of the form. Then add the column totals for each page of the log that you have filled out. Figure 8 is an example of one page of a completed Young Adult Library Survey Log.
7. Now turn to the Young Adult Library Survey Summary (Form 17). Follow the directions to calculate the **Young Adult Fill Rate.** You also will be able to calculate the **Homework Fill Rate** on the form from the data collected if you have used the forms exactly as described. Figure 9 is an example of a completed Young Adult Library Survey Summary.
8. The form also provides data about circulation of library materials to young adults, data that are often unavailable through normal circulation reporting systems. See the instructions for **Circulation of Materials per Young Adult** about calculating this measure, if you need additional information.

Interpreting and Using the Data

1. The fill rates don't tell why a patron's search was unsuccessful. They simply indicate the probability that a search by a young adult will be successful.
2. Some libraries have added an additional line that asks, "Did a librarian assist you today?" The answer to this question may provide a little more evidence to help in interpreting the results.
3. It is sometimes enlightening to examine Materials Use measures along with Materials Availability measures. You might find that your **Circulation of Materials per Young Adult** is very high, while the **Young Adult Fill Rate** is quite low. This discrepancy might indicate a very busy library in which the collection is so heavily used that individual patrons are sometimes frustrated in their searches for specific items. On the other hand, an underused library might have very high fill rates. In this library a few patrons are able to find much of what they want.
4. The information on the Young Adult Library Survey forms may give you some clues about why your fill rates are high or low because the young adult has a space to write in what he or she was looking for, as well as whether it was found.
5. If you want to increase **Young Adult Fill Rates:**
   - Reevaluate your collection development policy to see if it meets the needs of your current young adult patrons.
   - Make your collection easier to use by putting up more effective signs or arranging it differently.
   - Offer more effective reference and readers' advisory services to young adults.
6. If you are concerned about what seem to be low fill rates and are unable to figure out their cause, try conducting some focus groups with young adult library users to find out more about their experiences when they try to find something in the library.

	(1) Title, subject, author				(2) Browsing		(3) Other	
	(a) Sought for school		*(b)* Not for school		*(a)* Browsers	*(b)* Found something	*(a)* Other	*(b)* Refused, blank, or missing
Form Number	*(c)* Found	*(d)* Not found	*(e)* Found	*(f)* Not found				
1	—	—	—	—	—	—	—	1
2	—	—	—	—	1	1	—	—
3	—	—	—	—	1	0	—	—
4	1	0	1	1	—	—	—	—
5	2	1	—	—	—	—	—	—
6	—	—	—	—	—	—	1	—
7	—	—	—	—	—	—	1	—
8	3	0	—	—	—	—	—	—
9	0	1	1	0	—	—	—	—
10	1	0	1	0	—	—	—	—
11	0	1	0	1	—	—	—	—
12	2	0	1	0	—	—	—	—
13	—	—	—	—	1	1	—	—
14	—	—	—	—	1	1	—	—
15	—	—	—	—	—	—	1	—
16	1	1	—	—	—	—	—	—
TOTAL	10	4	4	2	4	3	3	1
	School items found	School items not found	Nonschool items found	Nonschool items not found	Number of browsers	Browsers finding something	Other	Not usable

Figure 8. Worked Example of Form 16: Young Adult Library Survey Log

1. Number of questionnaires handed out (1) 112
2. Questionnaires returned with usable title/subject/author or browsing answers (total of questions minus the total of columns 3a and 3b on Form 16) (2) 102
3. Questionnaires with only "other" question checked (total of column 3a) (3) 3
4. Usable questionnaires (subtotal of lines 2 and 3) (4) 105
5. Questionnaires marked "refused," with no usable responses, or never returned (total of 3b) (5) 7
6. Response rate (line 4 divided by line 1) (6) .94

Young Adult Fill Rate

7. Title/subject/authors sought (total of columns 1c, d, e, and f) (7) 93
8. Title/subject/authors found (total of columns 1c and 1e) (8) 82
9. Title/subject/authors fill rate (line 8 divided by line 7) (9) .88
10. Number of browsers (total of column 2a) (10) 10
11. Number of browsers finding something (total of column 2b) (11) 7
12. Browsing fill rate (line 11 divided by line 10) (12) .70
13. **Young Adult Fill Rate**

    (13a) total of line 8 and line 11 (13a) 89

    (13b) total of line 7 and line 10 (13b) 103

    (13c) 13a divided by 13b (13c) .86

Homework Fill Rate

14. Title/subject/authors sought for school (total of column 1c and 1d) (14) 70
15. Title/subject/authors sought for school and found (total of column 1c) (15) 62
16. **Homework Fill Rate** (line 15 divided by line 14) (16) .89

Figure 9. Worked Example of Form 17: Young Adult Library Survey Summary

Further Possibilities

1. **Young Adult Fill Rate** measures the probability of a young adult having success finding an item anywhere in the collection. You might want to structure a survey that measures search success in only the young adult collection.
2. The following output measure, **Homework Fill Rate,** is an example of a specialized fill rate. You might think of others that you would like to design.

Homework Fill Rate

Definition:	Proportion of successful searches by young adults for information and/or library materials to use with homework assignments.
Calculation:	Number of successful searches for homework materials divided by all searches for homework materials.
Data Collection:	A survey of young adult users taken during one typical week during the school year.
Example:	During a typical week during the school year, one library found that young adults searched for 267 items for school use. Of these, 180 searches were successful. Divide 180 by 267 to find the **Homework Fill Rate**. The figure is .67, or 67 percent. There is a 67 percent chance that a young adult's search for a library item needed for homework use was successful during the year. $\frac{180}{267} = .67$

Collecting the Data and Calculating the Measure

1. See the previous measure, **Young Adult Fill Rate,** for directions on administering the survey and calculating the measure. You may calculate this measure from the data from one typical week during the school year; it is not necessary to collect data during the summer months when school is not in session.
2. Calculate the measure from data on the Young Adult Library Survey Summary (Form 17), as directed.

Interpreting and Using the Data

1. If your library has adopted Formal Education Support Services as one of its roles, you will be interested in the results from this output measure. It tells you how well your collection and services support the curriculum needs of your young adult patrons.
2. If the middle schools and high schools in your community have excellent school library media centers, you may find that you do not need to be as aggressive about meeting curriculum needs of young adults. You may find that you have low **Homework Fill Rates** because you have not really tried to meet the needs of the few young adults who come to you instead of their school libraries for homework materials.
3. You may want to work with the school library media centers in your community to develop collections and services that are complementary to each other to meet the needs of the young people in your community.

Information Services Measures

Libraries offer information services to help patrons use resources and to provide answers to questions. Young adults are major consumers of both reference and readers' advisory services. There are two output measures that address these services:

Young Adult Information Transactions per Young Adult
Young Adult Information Transaction Completion Rate

Both of these measures apply only to transactions between library staff and young adults, not to instances when young adults find information with no assistance.

If you use the data collection method suggested here, you will have the data to calculate both measures. The young adult output measures correspond to both **Reference Transactions per Capita** and **Reference Completion Rate** from *Output Measures in Public Libraries,* second edition, and the Information Services measures in *Output Measures for Public Library Service to Children.*

Many libraries will be interested in capturing data about information services for all three age levels—children, young adult, and adult. These will be particularly important measures for libraries with a Reference Center focus. If these libraries choose to gather information service data for each age level separately, they will be counting information transactions for five weeks during the year. An alternative would be to use the same form to collect the data for all ages during two sample weeks, one in summer and one during the school year.

A *young adult information transaction* is a contact between a young adult user and a library staff member who provides help with or knowledge, interpretation, or instruction in the use of an information source. The librarian also may simply answer the young adult's information question. Information sources include materials in all formats, as well as library catalogs and other holdings records including:

- telephone, mail, and fax requests for reference and readers' advisory assistance—if you can determine whether the request was made by a young adult—as well as in-person requests

- requests for assistance using the catalog, but not simple mechanical questions

  Count

  "How do I find books about drug abuse in the catalog?"

  or

  "How do I find an author's name in the catalog?"

  but not

  "Can I make a copy of the page?"
- questions of fact
  "Where did Anne Frank die?"
- requests for help in finding facts
  "Can you help me find some information about Anne Frank?"
- general or specific requests for something to read
  "Where can I find books by R. L. Stine?"
  "Help me find a classic for a book report."
- requests for information and referral
  "Where can I find an algebra tutor?"
  "How can I find out about summer jobs?"
  database searches

Young adult information transactions do *not* include:

- simple directional questions
  "Where is the drinking fountain?"
- questions about rules and policies
  "Why can't I check out videos?"
- questions about library programs
  "When does the wrestling program start?"
  "How do I sign up to be a teen volunteer?"

However, in many cases, questions like the preceding excluded types may develop into true reference inquiries in the course of the ensuing dialogue between the young adult and the librarian. If an information interaction changes into a reference inquiry, it should be counted.

Young Adult Information Transactions per Young Adult

Definition:	Number of information transactions by young adults or adults acting on their behalf per young adult in the community served.
Calculation:	Divide the ANNUAL NUMBER OF YOUNG ADULT INFORMATION TRANSACTIONS by the YOUNG ADULT POPULATION OF LEGAL SERVICE AREA.
Data Collection:	Library staff tallies questions during two one-week sample periods, one in summer and one during the school year.
Example:	During a typical week in summer, 100 information transactions were initiated by young adult library users and by adults acting on their behalf. Multiply 100 by 12 to get the Summer Young Adult Information Transactions (1,200). During a typical sample week during the school year, 200 information transactions were initiated by young adult users and by adults acting on their behalf. Multiply 200 by 40 to get the School Year Young Adult Transactions (8,000). Add the Summer Young Adult Transactions (1,200) and the School Year Young Adult Transactions (8,000) to get the ANNUAL NUMBER OF YOUNG ADULT INFORMATION TRANSACTIONS (9,200). In this community, the YOUNG ADULT POPULATION OF LEGAL SERVICE AREA is 2,000. To find the **Young Adult Information Transactions per Young Adult,** divide the ANNUAL NUMBER OF YOUNG ADULT INFORMATION TRANSACTIONS (9,200) by the YOUNG ADULT POPULATION OF LEGAL SERVICE AREA (2,000). The measure is 4.6. On average, young adults in this community initiated 4.6 information transactions with library staff during the year.

$$\frac{(100 \times 12) + (200 \times 40)}{2{,}000} = 4.6$$

Young Adult Information Transaction Completion Rate

Definition: Percentage of information transactions by young adults or by adults acting on their behalf that are completed successfully, in the judgment of the librarian, on the same day that the question is asked.

Calculation: Divide ANNUAL NUMBER OF YOUNG ADULT INFORMATION TRANSACTIONS COMPLETED by the ANNUAL NUMBER OF YOUNG ADULT INFORMATION TRANSACTIONS.

Data Collection: Library staff tallies information transactions during two one-week sample periods, one in summer and one during the school year.

Example: During a typical week in summer, young adult library users and adults acting on their behalf asked a total of 100 questions at all public service desks. Of these questions, 10 were directional or program-related questions and not counted as information transactions. There were 3 questions redirected to other departments or libraries, and 5 questions were not answered or completed on the same day they were asked. The Number of Young Adult Summer Information Transactions Completed was 82. Subtract the number of directional questions (10) from the total number of questions asked (100) to find the Young Adult Summer Information Transactions; the answer is 90. To calculate the Young Adult Summer Information Transaction Completion Rate, divide the Number of Young Adult Summer Information Transactions Completed (82) by the Young Adult Summer Information Transactions (90); the result is .91, or 91 percent.

During a typical week during the school year, 170 questions were asked by young adults. Of these, 20 were directional, mechanical, or program-related questions; 10 questions were redirected to other departments or libraries; and 10 questions were not answered on the same day they were asked. The Number of Young Adult School Year Information Transactions Completed was 130. Subtract the number of directional questions (20) from the total number of questions asked (170) to find the Young Adult School Year Information Transactions (150). To calculate the Young Adult School Year Information Transaction Completion Rate, divide the Number of Young Adult School Year Information Transactions Completed (130) by the Young Adult School Year Information Transactions (150); the answer is .87, or 87 percent.

To calculate the annual **Young Adult Information Transaction Completion Rate,** convert the Young Adult Summer Information Transaction Rate and the Young Adult School Year Transaction Completion Rate to decimals. Multiply the Young Adult School Year Information Transaction Completion Rate (.87) by 3 to get a weighted average (2.61). Add the weighted school year average and the Young Adult Summer Information Transaction Completion Rate (.91). The total is 3.52. Divide the total by 4 to get the **Young Adult Information Transaction Completion Rate** of .88, or 688 percent. There was an 83 percent chance that a young adult's information transaction (or that of an adult acting on his or her behalf) was successfully completed on the day that it was asked.

$$\frac{82}{90} = .91 \qquad \frac{130}{150} = .87 \qquad \frac{.91 + (3 \times .87)}{4} = .88$$

Collecting the Data

1. Select a typical week to collect your data.
2. If, after tallying reference transactions for one week, you have not counted at least 100 separate transactions, keep counting for one more week. You need to have at least 100 transactions for the sample size to be meaningful.
3. You may collect data for the **Young Adult Information Transaction Completion Rate** at the same time that you collect data for the **Young Adult Information Transactions per Young Adult** measure.
4. During the sample period, have staff at all service points record all information transactions initiated by young adult library users and by adults acting on their behalf on Form 18, Young Adult Information Transaction Tally Sheet. They should count at all times during the week, not just in selected periods. Number all tally sheets before you distribute them so you'll be sure to get them all back.
5. The Young Adult Information Transaction Tally Sheet includes a summary of directions for staff, but they may still get confused about what kind of question to record in what space. They also may be uncertain about how to identify a young adult library user. Cover these issues in your staff training.
6. Remind staff that multiple questions from a single patron should be recorded as multiple hash marks on the form.
7. Sometimes a parent accompanies a young adult to the library and speaks on behalf of the young adult or comes in alone to get materials for the young person. Middle school and secondary teachers also request help in getting materials that are then used by groups of teenagers. These transactions should be recorded as young adult information transactions because young adults are the end users of the materials. It is not always possible to determine who is going to be the ultimate recipient of the information, but when the reference librarian can tell from the context of the question or the interview that a teenager is the end user, these transactions should be recorded as Young Adult Information Transactions.

Calculating the Measures

1. To calculate **Young Adult Information Transactions per Young Adult** using two sample weeks, one in summer and one during the school year, collect data as described for a typical week in summer and a typical week during the school year.
2. Multiply the number of Young Adult Information Transactions from the summer week by 12 to get the number of Young Adult Summer Information Transactions.
3. Multiply the number of Young Adult Information Transactions from the school year week by 40 to get the number of Young Adult School Year Information Transactions.
4. Add the Young Adult Summer Information Transactions and the Young Adult School Year Information Transactions to get the ANNUAL NUMBER OF YOUNG ADULT INFORMATION TRANSACTIONS.
5. Divide the ANNUAL NUMBER OF YOUNG ADULT INFORMATION TRANSACTIONS by the YOUNG ADULT POPULATION OF LEGAL SERVICE AREA to determine **Young Adult Information Transactions per Young Adult.**
6. To calculate **Young Adult Information Transaction Completion Rate,** collect data for a typical week in summer and a typical week in winter as described. For each week, tally the number of directional questions, the number of questions redirected, the number of questions not answered, the number of questions answered (Young Adult Information Transactions Completed), and the total number of questions asked (Form 18).
7. Subtract the directional questions from the total number of questions asked to get the number of Young Adult Information Transactions.
8. Divide the Number of Young Adult Information Transactions Completed by the number of Young Adult Information Transactions to get the Young Adult Information Transaction Completion Rate for each week. (The rate will be expressed as a decimal or as a percentage.)
9. Multiply the Young Adult School Year Information Transaction Completion Rate by 3 to get a weighted average. Add the weighted average to the Young Adult Summer Information Completion Rate and divide by 4 to get the annual **Young Adult Information Transaction Completion Rate.**

Interpreting and Using the Data

1. The **Young Adult Information Transactions per Young Adult** measure tells you the average number of questions asked by young adults or adults acting on their behalf for each

young adult living in the community. **Young Adult Information Transaction Completion Rate** tells you the percentage of those questions that are answered, in the opinion of the staff handling the transaction. It does not take into account the patron's opinion about whether the transaction was successful.

2. A high **Young Adult Information Transactions per Young Adult** shows a high level of interaction between staff and young adults. This high level may mean that the staff is friendly, approachable, and competent. On the other hand, it may mean that the library is difficult to use, that the staff members haven't tried to teach young adults to use the library independently, or that the young adults lack information-seeking skills.
3. A low **Young Adult Information Transactions per Young Adult** combined with a high **Circulation of Materials per Young Adult** may show that the library is used primarily for popular materials and browsing, with little or no staff assistance being required. This finding might be expected for a library with a Popular Materials Library role.
4. A low **Young Adult Information Transaction Completion Rate** may mean that staff are inexperienced in answering young adults' questions or that the library does not support the information needs of young adults in the community. It may also indicate a gap between the library's perception of its role and young adults' expectations of the library. For example, young adults may expect to find homework help in the library, while staff expects young adults to do their homework unassisted or with the help of school librarians.
5. If you want to increase the **Young Adult Information Transactions per Young Adult,** consider these approaches:
   - Let young adults know the kinds of informational assistance you can provide.
   - Increase the visibility of your information service desks.
   - Encourage staff to be more proactive about offering assistance to young adults instead of waiting for them to ask for help.
6. If you want to increase the **Young Adult Information Transaction Completion Rate**:
   - Train staff in effective ways of communicating with young adults.
   - Train staff in use of reference and readers' advisory reference tools relevant to young adults.
   - Increase staffing at public service desks.
   - Evaluate the collection to see if it meets young adults' information needs.

Further Possibilities

1. Collect data for all age levels—children, young adult, and adult—during your sample weeks. Form 19, Children, Young Adult, and Adult Information Transaction Tally Sheet, can be used for this compilation. To help staff distinguish among the three age levels, use signs such as the following at all public service desks:

   Reference survey this week.
   Please tell us your age group:
   Child (1–11)
   Young Adult (12–18)
   Adult (over 18)

   Calculate information transaction rates for each age level as the instructions on Form 19 indicate.
2. Analyze total information transactions by time period to document work load.

Programming Measures

Programming refers to the planned events that are sponsored by libraries to introduce library services, provide information or entertainment, or promote the library. Programs may take place in the library or at some other location. The library is a primary sponsor of the event, however, if it contributes its name, time, money, space, or people to the planning and presentation of the program.

There are two output measures for programming.

Young Adult Program Attendance per Young Adult measures attendance by people of all ages at library programs planned for a young adult audience.

Program Attendance per Young Adult, on the other hand, measures attendance by young adults at any library program.

Programs may include lectures, panel discussions, concerts, author visits, library tours, and events for groups such as school classes or clubs. Note that this definition is somewhat different from the definition in *Output Measures for Public Library Service for Children,* which excludes visits by school classes from the programming measure. In that manual, class visits are counted separately for a separate output measure, **Class Visit Rate.**

Young Adult Program Attendance per Young Adult

Definition:	Annual attendance at young adult programs per young adult in the community served.
Calculation:	ANNUAL YOUNG ADULT PROGRAM ATTENDANCE divided by the YOUNG ADULT POPULATION OF LEGAL SERVICE AREA.
Data Collection:	Count the audience at all programs during the year for which the primary audience is young adults.
Example:	There were 480 people who attended young adult programs at the library during the year; the ANNUAL YOUNG ADULT PROGRAM ATTENDANCE is 480. There are 412 young adults in the community. Divide 480 by 412 to find the **Young Adult Program Attendance per Young Adult**: 1.16. On average, each young adult in the community attended at least one young adult program at the library during the year. $\frac{480}{412} = 1.16$

Collecting the Data and Calculating the Measure

1. Count attendance at all programs planned for young adults. Count adults and children as well as young adults.
2. Do not use sample weeks for this measure. Count attendance at *all* young adult programs during the year.
3. If you do not already have a way to keep a record of young adult program attendance, you may use Form 20, Young Adult Program Attendance Log.
4. At the end of the year, total the attendance from all young adult programs to find the ANNUAL YOUNG ADULT PROGRAM ATTENDANCE. Divide by the YOUNG ADULT POPULATION OF LEGAL SERVICE AREA to find the **Young Adult Program Attendance per Young Adult.**

Interpreting and Using the Data

1. This measure indicates only the average attendance at young adult programs by young adults in the community. It does not account for young adults who are repeat attendees. The unit of analysis is attendance, not attendees. In fact, you will count the attendance each week of the same regular book discussion participants. Each book discussion session is a separate program for purposes of this measure.
2. This measure also does not indicate young adult satisfaction with programs, although high attendance probably indicates more satisfaction than low attendance. If you want to find out more about the satisfaction level, use attendee surveys, interviews, or focus groups.
3. If you want to increase **Young Adult Program Attendance per Young Adult:**
   - Have more young adult programs.
   - Have more-appealing young adult programs.
   - Repeat successful programs.
   - Publicize your programs more effectively.
   - Offer programs that attract large crowds.
   - Offer several sessions of programs geared to smaller groups, such as book discussions.

- Target particular groups of young adults, such as soccer fans or graduating seniors.
- Involve young adults in both the planning and publicizing of programs.

Further Possibilities

1. Keep separate counts of attendance at different kinds of young adult programs, such as author visits or writing classes.
2. Relate young adult program attendance to other output measures, such as **Building Use by Young Adults.**

Program Attendance per Young Adult

Definition:	Annual attendance at all library programs by young adults per young adult in the legal service area.
Calculation:	ANNUAL PROGRAM ATTENDANCE BY YOUNG ADULTS divided by YOUNG ADULT POPULATION OF LEGAL SERVICE AREA.
Data Collection:	Count attendance by young adults at all library programs during the year.
Example:	There were 580 young adults who attended library programs during the year; the ANNUAL PROGRAM ATTENDANCE BY YOUNG ADULTS is 580. There are 800 young adults in the community. Divide the ANNUAL PROGRAM ATTENDANCE BY YOUNG ADULTS (580) by 800 to find the **Program Attendance per Young Adult**: .73. On average, 73 percent of the young adults in the community attended a library program during the year. $\frac{800}{580} = .73$

Collecting the Data and Calculating the Measure

1. Count all young adults attending all library programs during the year. The people doing the attendance count must be able to identify young adults by sight. Accurate counting requires the cooperation of all library staff who present programs. The children's librarian, for example, must report young adults attending family storytimes. Adult librarians must report young adults attending adult programs such as poetry readings.
2. Do not use sample weeks; count young adult attendance at all programs throughout the year.
3. Record the data on a form such as Form 21, Program Attendance by Young Adults Log.
4. To calculate the measure, total all young adult attendance figures from the Program Attendance by Young Adults Log during the year to find the ANNUAL PROGRAM ATTENDANCE BY YOUNG ADULTS. Divide by the YOUNG ADULT POPULATION OF LEGAL SERVICE AREA to find the **Program Attendance per Young Adult** figure.

Interpreting and Using the Data

1. This measure is more inclusive than **Young Adult Program Attendance per Young Adult.** It includes attendance by young adults at young adult programs as well as all other programs.
2. Compare this measure with other general young adult use measures such as **Circulation of Materials per Young Adult.**

Community Relations Measures

The output measures in this section give indicators of some of the work done on behalf of young adults with groups, individuals, and organizations outside the library. There are no comparable measures in *Output Measures for Public Libraries,* second edition. *Output Measures for Public Library Service to Children* includes similar measures.

Young Adult School Contact Rate measures the annual number of contacts made by library staff with schools serving young adults relative to the total number of schools serving young adults.

Annual Number of Young Adult Community Contacts is the total number of contacts in a year made by library staff with community organizations, institutions, or individuals on behalf of public library service to young adults.

Young Adult School Contact Rate

Definition:	Annual number of contacts with schools serving young adults per total number of schools serving young adults.
Calculation:	ANNUAL NUMBER OF YOUNG ADULT SCHOOL CONTACTS divided by TOTAL NUMBER OF YOUNG ADULT SCHOOLS.
Data Collection:	Count all contacts by library staff with schools serving young adults. Count all schools serving young adults.
Example:	There are 2 public middle schools, 1 public high school, 1 independent high school, and 1 Catholic high school in the community. The TOTAL NUMBER OF YOUNG ADULT SCHOOLS is 5. Library staff visited each school twice during the year, once to contact the school librarian and once to publicize the library's young adult poetry festival. In addition, the young adult librarian visited 6 classes at one middle school to give book talks, and she met twice with the principal of the public high school to discuss after-school behavior problems at the library. The ANNUAL NUMBER OF YOUNG ADULT SCHOOL CONTACTS is 18. Divide the ANNUAL NUMBER OF YOUNG ADULT SCHOOL CONTACTS (18) by the TOTAL NUMBER OF YOUNG ADULT SCHOOLS (5) to find the **Young Adult School Contact Rate**: 3.6. On average, library staff made 3.6 contacts with each school serving young adults during the year. $\frac{18}{5} = 3.6$

Collecting the Data and Calculating the Measure

1. You will need to do a census of schools serving young adults in the community if you do not already know the number. This figure is the TOTAL NUMBER OF YOUNG ADULT SCHOOLS. Note that some young adult schools may also serve children, if their grade configuration is kindergarten through eighth grade, for example. For the purposes of this output measure, it is a young adult school if *any portion* of its student body is in the age range you define as young adult.
2. Keep a record of all visits made to schools serving young adults. Use Form 22, Young Adult School Contact Log, if you do not have a procedure in place for keeping this count. A contact can be an actual visit or a telephone call. Telephone calls should involve substantive content, however.
3. At the end of the year, count all contacts made with schools serving young adults to find the ANNUAL NUMBER OF YOUNG ADULT SCHOOL CONTACTS.
4. Divide the ANNUAL NUMBER OF YOUNG ADULT SCHOOL CONTACTS by the TOTAL

NUMBER OF YOUNG ADULT SCHOOLS to find the Young Adult School Contact Rate.

Interpreting and Using the Data

1. This measure is one indicator of the library's relationship with the major institution serving young adults in most communities. It should be important to most libraries that have a commitment to serving young adults and of particular concern to libraries with a Formal Education Support Service role.
2. Make elected officials aware of the work the library is doing with the schools in the community.
3. Link this data with other output measures such as **Young Adult Homework Fill Rate.**

Further Possibilities

Count contacts with individual home schooling families or with home school organizations for a Young Adult Home School Contact Rate.

Annual Number of Young Adult Community Contacts

Definition:	Annual number of community contacts made by library staff with organizations and individuals serving youth or on behalf of public library service to young adults.
Calculation:	Count number of young adult community contacts.
Data Collection:	Keep a record of all young adult community contacts.
Example:	During one year, the young adult librarian published 5 press releases in the local paper. He also attended 4 meetings of the youth coalition, 2 meetings of the middle school parents' organization, and 1 meeting of the Rotary Club. He met 2 times with staff at the Teen Post and 1 time with staff at the recreation center. The library director attended 2 meetings of the youth coalition and spoke 1 time with the police chief about graffiti problems at the library. The children's librarian gave 4 talks to classes of pregnant teenagers at the health center. Several staff appeared 1 time on a local television program promoting summer library programs for children and young adults. **The Annual Number of Young Adult Community Contacts** is 23.

Collecting the Data and Calculating the Measure

1. Keep a log of all community contacts made by the young adult librarian or on behalf of public library service to young adults by any member of the library staff. A contact may be an actual visit, a substantive telephone call, a media appearance, or a published press release.
2. Use Form 23, Young Adult Community Contact Log, if you do not now have a procedure for keeping track of young adult community contacts.
3. At the end of the year, simply count all young adult community contacts to find the **Annual Number of Young Adult Community Contacts.**

Using the Data and Interpreting the Results

1. The work activities that are reflected in this output measure are a means for acquiring community information and developing good will for the library. The contacts themselves also may be considered "ends" if the library has as one objective the development of more community partners.
2. Libraries with the roles of Community Information Services or Community Activity Services will be particularly interested in this measure.

Youth Participation Measures

Youth participation measures voluntary participation by young adults in library activities other than normal usage of the library such as checking out books, using reference services, or attending programs. Youth participants volunteer their services to assist with decision-making or service-delivery activities such as those indicated in the following example. Court referrals should be counted even though their participation may not appear to be voluntary. In fact, young adults referred by the court usually have some discretion over the location of their community service and, thus, should be considered as youth participants in this case.

Most organizations that use volunteers see them as an input, or resource, rather than as an output. However, the importance of encouraging positive societal and economic roles as part of healthy young adult social and emotional development has been so well-documented that youth participation can reasonably be viewed as an output of library service to young adults. Youth advocates will see the creation of opportunities for participation by young adults as a key element in their overall plan of library service to young adults.

Young Adult Participation Rate

Definition: Number of young adults who participate in voluntary service activities at the library in a given year relative to the number of young adults living in the community.

Calculation: ANNUAL NUMBER OF YOUTH PARTICIPANTS divided by YOUNG ADULT POPULATION OF LEGAL SERVICE AREA.

Data Collection: Librarian keeps a record of all young adults who voluntarily participate in decision making and/or service delivery activities.

Example: During one year, 22 young adults did the 10 hours of community service required by their school at the public library. Their work consisted primarily of reshelving materials and processing paperback books. Also, 2 young adults were referred by the court for 20 hours of community service. There were 15 young adults who participated in book reviewing activities and 10 young adults who participated as members of the library's youth advisory council. An additional 7 young adults helped the members of the youth advisory council and the youth services librarian with the planning and staffing of a library booth at the recreation department's summer youth fair. Furthermore, 8 young adults volunteered to assist with the children's summer reading program, and 5 young adults volunteered as tutors for the homework center. The ANNUAL NUMBER OF YOUTH PARTICIPANTS is 69. The YOUNG ADULT POPULATION OF LEGAL SERVICE AREA (number of young adults living in the library's service area) is 834. To find the **Young Adult Participation Rate,** divide the ANNUAL NUMBER OF YOUTH PARTICIPANTS (69) by the YOUNG ADULT POPULATION OF LEGAL SERVICE AREA (834). The result is .08, or 8 percent. In this year, 8 percent of the young adults in this community participated in voluntary service activities at the library.

$$\frac{69}{834} = .08$$

Collecting the Data

1. One library staff member should be responsible for keeping a record of youth participants. Ordinarily, this person would be the youth services librarian. In some cases, it might be an administrative assistant who is assigned the responsibility for statistical reporting or a volunteer coordinator. Whoever is responsible for this measure should be sure to collect information about youth participants from all departments in the library. Youth participants may be working in such diverse sites as tech-

nical services, circulation, or the children's department. All young adults serving as youth volunteers or youth participants in any capacity in any area of the library should be counted for this measure.

2. The names of all youth participants in the given year are accumulated and tallied for the ANNUAL NUMBER OF YOUTH PARTICIPANTS. If you do not presently have a mechanism for gathering this information, you may want to use Form 24, Individual Youth Participant Record, as a way of keeping track of your individual youth participants and Form 25, Youth Participation Tally Sheet, as a way of tabulating the ANNUAL NUMBER OF YOUTH PARTICIPANTS. Figure 10 is an example of a completed Individual Youth Participant Record.

Calculating the Measure

1. Use Form 25, Youth Participation Tally Sheet, to count the ANNUAL NUMBER OF YOUTH PARTICIPANTS. Young adults who participate in more than one activity are counted only once for this measure. See Figure 11 for an example of a completed Form 25, Youth Participation Tally Sheet.
2. Divide the ANNUAL NUMBER OF YOUTH PARTICIPANTS by YOUNG ADULT POPULATION OF LEGAL SERVICE AREA. The answer will be a decimal. Express this as a percentage to indicate the **Young Adult Participation Rate.**

Interpreting and Using the Data

1. The **Young Adult Participation Rate** will probably be lower than some of the other measures of young adult usage of the library. This low figure may be considered consistent with voluntary participation in all sectors of society. A spectrum of individual library usage from low to high might look something like this:

Non-use	LOW
Occasional use of collection or services (1–2 times a year)	↑
Moderate use of collection or services (3–10 times a year)	
Heavy use of collection or services (More than 11 times a year)	
Voluntary participation in decision making or service delivery activities	↓ HIGH

Usage at the higher end of the scale requires more personal commitment than usage at the lower end of the scale, and fewer people will want to make that commitment.

2. Do not assume, however, that youth participants are also heavy users of library materials or services. While there is often a correlation between library usage and voluntary participation, some young adults may choose to volunteer at the library to meet a community service obligation at their school, for example, and these individuals may rarely make use of the library's resources.
3. If you want to increase the **Young Adult Participation Rate:**

- Evaluate the tasks that you are assigning to young adult volunteers.

  Are they meaningful and varied? Does the young adult understand how important these tasks are to the library operations? Are the young adults learning any skills, attitudes, or values that will be useful to them in other areas of life?

- Evaluate the quality of supervision given to youth participants. Are you providing appropriate amounts of structure *and* flexibility? Are you providing good feedback? Are you demonstrating your appreciation for the services provided?

- Monitor the behavior of other library staff toward the youth participants. Are the young adults made to feel welcome and needed?

- Use the focus group and/or interview techniques discussed in Part 2 to get feedback from young adults about why they do or do not choose to participate in voluntary service at the library.

- Be sure that local schools know that you offer volunteer service opportunities to young adults.

- Advertise your participation opportunities and activities through local media, youth organizations, churches, etc.

- See the Sources for Additional Information at the end of Part 2 for some guides to volunteer management in general and youth participation in particular.

Name Vivian Montero

Address 3560 Oakwood

Venice

Telephone —

Birth Date 5-13-80 School Venice H.S.

Library Participation Activities

Date	Activity	Total Hours
7-15-95	Summer Reading Helper	2
7-22-95	" " "	2
7-29-95	" " "	2
8-6-95	" " "	2
8-13-95	" " "	2
8-20-95	" " "	2
8-27-95	" " "	4
9-20-95	Youth Advisory Council	2
11-15-95	" " "	2
11-18-95	Friends Book Sale	5
	moved, 12-95	

Figure 10. Worked Example of Form 24: Individual Youth Participant Record

Name	Activities	Total Hours
Vivian Montero	Y. A. C.	4
	Summer Reading	16
	Book Sale	5
Aidan Stockard	Y. A. C.	16
	Tutoring - (community service)	12
Tyrone Taylor	Y. A. C.	8
Sandy Trevino	Summer Reading	10
Judy Washington	Y. A. C.	6
Latoya Washington	Y. A. C.	6
Bob Yoshimoto	Y. A. C.	12
	Tutoring	10
Lanny Young	Book sale	4
Craig Young	Book sale	4

Figure 11. Worked Example of Form 25: Youth Participation Tally Sheet

Further Possibilities

1. If your library keeps track of the number of adult volunteers, calculate the Adult Participation Rate and compare it with the **Young Adult Participation Rate**.
2. Share your data with other community agencies who have youth participation programs. Consider calculating a Community Young Adult Participation Rate.

Annual Number of Young Adult Volunteer Hours

Definition:	Total number of hours worked by young adult volunteers in the library during the year.
Calculation:	Count the total number of hours worked by young adult volunteers.
Data Collection:	Keep a record of young adult volunteer hours.
Example:	From the Youth Participation Tally Sheet, Form 25, the young adult librarian determined that the 10 young adults who had participated in voluntary activities at the library during the year had contributed a total of 314 hours. **The Annual Number of Young Adult Volunteer Hours** is 314.

Collecting and Calculating the Data

1. Use Form 24, Individual Youth Participant Record, to keep track of individual volunteer hours. Summarize the data on Form 25, Youth Participation Tally Sheet, at the end of the year.
2. Count all volunteer hours listed on the Youth Participation Tally Sheet to find the **Annual Number of Young Adult Volunteer Hours**.

Interpreting and Using the Data

1. See the section on **Young Adult Participation Rate** for ideas about increasing the number of young adult volunteer hours.
2. Compare the **Annual Number of Young Adult Volunteer Hours** with the Annual Number of Adult Volunteer Hours.
3. Multiply the **Annual Number of Young Adult Volunteer Hours** by the minimum wage or your lowest hourly salary rate to find the economic worth of the labor contributed by young adults.

Some Last Words of Encouragement

Implementing output measures for a segment of the library population such as young adults is a task that yields immediate and some long-term satisfactions. In the short term, the library gains useful statistics that enable staff to better understand the results of their work. The output measures provide quantitative evidence of the library's progress toward reaching goals and objectives that can be used in allocating resources and focusing staff efforts.

The long-term satisfactions and benefits should include improved library services to an important segment of the community and the user populations. Young people at the end of the twentieth century are struggling to adulthood at a time when the promise of the information age has yet to be met. Information proliferates. It is available through books; increasing numbers of magazines published for increasingly specialized markets; radio; network, public, and cable television; electronic databases; electronic networks; and many other venues. There is little evidence to suggest that young adults are able to maneuver through this maze of information providers with ease. Libraries have an increasing responsibility to provide road maps to the information superhighway as well as the more prosaic avenues to information and misinformation. *Output Measures and More: Planning and Evaluating Public Library Services for Young Adults* will help you evaluate your efforts.

The Young Adult Library Services Association is interested in knowing about your efforts with these young adult output measures. Please share your stories, your problems, and your successes with the YALSA office at ALA Headquarters, 50 E. Huron Street, Chicago, IL 60611.

APPENDIX A
Sample Interview and Focus Group Questions

Interview Schedule for Homework Center Users
(15 to 30 minutes)

Introduction

I'm trying to find out what young adults who use the homework center think of it. I have six questions to ask you, and it shouldn't take more than twenty minutes unless you have a whole lot to say. I need you to be as open and honest in your answers as you can be. You won't hurt my feelings if you say something bad about the homework center or the library. I wouldn't be asking if I didn't really want to know what you think. Okay? Here we go.

1. What kinds of homework do you do when you are using the homework center?
2. Why do you use the homework center?
3. In general, what do you think of the homework center?
4. What do you like best about it?
5. How would you improve it, make it more useful for you and other young adults?
6. What else should I know about the homework center?

Interview Schedule for Young Adult Users of the Young Adult Book Collection
(20 to 40 minutes)

Introduction

I'm trying to find out what young adults think about our collection of young adult books. That's the section of books over in the corner with the picture labels—"Horror," "Romance," etc. I know you might think we've done a really bad job with this collection, and if that's so, I need you to tell me. I won't be able to make improvements if you don't tell me what you like and don't like. You won't hurt my feelings if you say something critical. It's okay to say good things, too, if you really mean them. Depending on how much you have to say, we'll probably be talking for anywhere from twenty to forty minutes. Okay? Let's start.

1. Tell me about your experiences looking for books in the Young Adult Collection.

   What kinds of books do you look for?
   Can you usually find them?
   What do you do when you can't find any thing that appeals to you?

Follow-Up Questions

   Do you ever just stumble on a book that looks good and take it out just because the cover or the title is appealing?
   Do you ever ask a librarian to help you find a particular book or just a good book?
   What have been your experiences?
   (Note: if you are interested in getting reactions to particular kinds of books, magazines, or other materials, it is a good idea to have actual samples of the materials there for the participants to see.)

2. What do you think about the way the young adult collection is organized?

   How easy is it to find things?
   How would you change it to make it easier or more pleasant to use?

3. You've probably noticed that our young adult collection is quite small, just a browsing section really. What kinds of books would you add?

4. When you use the young adult collection, are you usually looking for books to read for pleasure or for school?

   Both?
   Some other reason?

5. What do you think about where the young adult collection is placed in the library?

   If we could move it anyplace, where would you suggest that it be?

6. What could we do to the young adult collection that would make you use it more or help you use it more easily?
7. What else would you like to tell me about the young adult collection?

Focus Group Questions for Young Adult Volunteers

(40 to 60 minutes)

Introduction

I'm going to ask you some questions about the volunteer work you do here at the library. There are no right or wrong answers. I hope you'll share your thoughts. I'm really interested in what you have to say. You won't hurt my feelings if you say something critical. It will help me to understand more about young adults who volunteer to work here. (*Alternative:* It will help me to improve our work with young adult volunteers.)

1. What is your definition of a "volunteer"?

   Would you call yourself a volunteer?
   Something else?

2. Do you remember why you decided to begin volunteering at the library?

   How long ago was that?
   About how often do you volunteer?
   How many hours a week?

3. What do you do when you volunteer at the library?
4. What kind of training did you get?

   How do they supervise your work?

5. What do you like best about it?

   Least?

6. How does your volunteer work help the library?
7. How does your volunteer work help or benefit you?
8. What else should I know to help me understand young adult volunteers in the library?

APPENDIX B

Blank Work Forms

1A Young Adult Community Information Data Sheet, Part A. Demographics

1B Young Adult Community Information Data Sheet, Part B. Organizations

2 Young Adult Community Organization Checklist

3 Young Adult Community Organization Data Sheet

4 Looking Around Summary Sheet

5 Selecting Library Roles Work Sheet

6 Young Adult Data Elements

7 Young Adult Library Visits Sampling Work Sheet

8 Young Adult Library Visits Tally Sheet

9 Building Use by Young Adults Data Collection Form

10 Furniture/Equipment Use by Young Adults Data Collection Form

11 Homework Center Visits Sampling Work Sheet

12 Homework Center Visits Tally Sheet

13 In-Library Use of Young Adult Materials Log

14 Young Adult In-Library Materials Use Tally Sheet

14A Young Adult In-Library Materials Use Tally Sheet, Spanish Translation

15 Young Adult Library Survey

15A Young Adult Library Survey, Spanish Translation

16 Young Adult Library Survey Log

17 Young Adult Library Survey Summary

18 Young Adult Information Transaction Tally Sheet

19 Children, Young Adult, and Adult Information Transaction Tally Sheet

20 Young Adult Program Attendance Log

21 Program Attendance by Young Adults Log

22 Young Adult School Contact Log

23 Young Adult Community Contact Log

24 Individual Youth Participant Record

25 Youth Participation Tally Sheet

Form 1A Young Adult Community Information Data Sheet

Part A. Demographics

1. Total population of community served (1) ______________

2. Total young adult population of community served (2) ______________

   Young adults definition:

   people between the ages of ____ and ____.

3. Percentage of population that is young adult (3) ______________

4. Per capita personal income (4) ______________

5. Percentage of persons under poverty level (5) ______________

6. Percentage of persons over 25 with:

   12 or more years of school completed (6) ______________

   16 or more years of school completed ______________

7. Racial/language/ethnic groups in the community

   List groups and give data where available

8. High school dropout rates (8) ______________

9. Standardized test scores for grades 8 and 12

10. Unemployment rate of community as a whole (10) ______________

11. Unemployment rate for people under 18 (11) ______________

Form 1B Young Adult Community Information Data Sheet

Part B. Organizations

1. Schools serving young adults:

   Public: Number _____ Enrollment _____

   Independent: Number _____ Enrollment _____

2. Estimated number of young adults in home schools (2) ________________

3. Number of religious groups or organizations (3) ________________

4. Number of public health clinics (4) ________________

5. Number of public recreation facilities (5) ________________

6. Number of public and nonprofit social service agencies serving youth (6) ________________

7. Number of youth gangs in community served (7) ________________

8. Estimated membership in youth gangs in community served (8) ________________

9. Clubs and membership organizations for young adults, excluding gangs—list:

10. Number of newspapers (10) ________________

11. Number of radio stations (11) ________________

12. Number of television stations (12) ________________

13. Other relevant trends, facts, or statistics about organizations:

Form 2 Young Adult Community Organization Checklist

Educational

☐ Public schools

☐ Independent Schools

☐ Church-affiliated schools

☐ Vocational schools

☐ Colleges, universities

☐ Home schools

☐ Tutoring programs

Cultural/Informational

☐ Museums

☐ Concert halls

☐ Music clubs

☐ Music, dance, or art classes

☐ Drama programs

☐ Mural programs

☐ Movie theaters

☐ Radio stations

☐ TV stations

☐ Community electronic networks

☐ Hot lines

☐ Environmental action groups

Sports/Recreation

☐ Swimming pools

☐ Amateur athletic leagues

☐ Ball fields

☐ Professional athletic teams

☐ Bicycle trails or velodromes

☐ Skateboard parks

☐ Gyms

☐ YMCA/YWCA

☐ Recreation centers

☐ Video arcades

☐ Martial arts schools

☐ Bowling alleys

Health/Social Service

☐ Hospitals

☐ Teen posts

☐ Girls/Boys Clubs

☐ Gang diversion programs

☐ Antigraffiti programs

☐ Juvenile halls

☐ Halfway houses

☐ Drug prevention programs

☐ Suicide prevention programs

☐ Homeless shelters

Form 3 Young Adult Community Organization Data Sheet

1. Name of organization
2. Address

3. Telephone Fax
4. Director's name
5. Key staff

6. Mission and major activities or services

7. Target population served

8. Source of funding
9. Newsletter? Yes _____ No _____ Will publicize library activities? Yes _____ No _____

   Deadlines

10. Previous history of cooperation with library

11. Last update of data sheet

Form 4 Looking Around Summary Sheet

Major Finding	Impact on Library Roles and Services	Opportunities	Possible Library Responses
1.			
2.			
3.			
4.			

Form 5 Selecting Library Roles Work Sheet

____
(Group)

Please allocate 100 points in the columns below. You need not divide points equally, and some roles may receive no points. Note that 20 of the 100 points have already been assigned to cover basic library activities and roles not selected for emphasis. In the first column, distribute the 80 remaining points based on how you see *current* library activities being implemented. In the second column, distribute the 8 points the way you feel library activities *should* be directed.

Role	Current Activities	Desired Commitment
Community activities services		
Community information services		
Formal education support services		
Independent learning services		
Popular materials library		
Preschoolers' door to learning		
Reference services		
Research center		
Miscellaneous activities and roles not selected for emphasis	20	20
Total points	100	100

Form 6 Young Adult Data Elements

Library ______________________________ Year ____________

1. Young Adult Population of Legal Service Area (1) ____________
2. Annual Number of Library Visits by Young Adults (2) ____________
3. Annual Number of Homework Center Visits (3) ____________
4. Annual Circulation of Young Adult Materials (4) ____________
5. Annual Circulation of Library Materials to Young Adults (5) ____________
6. Annual In-Library Use of Young Adult Materials (6) ____________
7. Annual In-Library Use of Library Materials by Young Adults (7) ____________
8. Young Adult Materials Holdings (8) ____________
9. Annual Number of Young Adult Information Transactions (9) ____________
10. Annual Number of Young Adult Information Transactions Completed (10) ____________
11. Annual Young Adult Program Attendance (11) ____________
12. Annual Program Attendance by Young Adults (12) ____________
13. Annual Number of Young Adult School Contacts (13) ____________
14. Total Number of Young Adult Schools (14) ____________
15. Annual Number of Youth Participants (15) ____________
16. Total Number of Young Adult Volunteer Hours (16) ____________

Form 7 Young Adult Library Visits Sampling Work Sheet

1. Total of all weekday morning visits made during the sample periods. (See Form 8, Section A.) (1) ________________
2. Number of weekday morning hours in the sample periods (e.g., 3 hours Monday morning + 3 hours Wednesday morning = 6). (2) ________________
3. (1) divided by (2) = average number of weekday morning library visits per hour. (3) ________________
4. Number of weekday morning hours the library is open each week. (4) ________________
5. (4) × (3) = the estimated number of weekday morning visits per week. (5) ________________
6. Repeat steps 1–5 for (a) early afternoon, (b) after school, (c) evening, (d) Saturday, and (e) Sunday hours, and record the estimated number of (6a) weekday early afternoon, (6b) weekday after school, (6c) weekday evening, (6d) Saturday, and (6e) Sunday visits per week.
   (6a) ________________
   (6b) ________________
   (6c) ________________
   (6d) ________________
   (6e) ________________
7. (5) + (6a) + (6b) + (6c) + (6d) + (6e) = the estimated number of young adult library visits each week. (7) ________________
8. Multiply (7) by 12 if this is a summer sample week. This is the estimated Summer Y.A. Library Visits count. If Summer Y.A. Library Visits count was taken earlier, record it in (8). (8) ________________
9. Multiply (7) by 40 if this is a school year sample week. This is the estimated School Year Y.A. Library Visits count. If School Year Y.A. Library Visits count was taken earlier, record it in (9). (9) ________________
10. Add (8) and (9) to get the estimated ANNUAL NUMBER OF LIBRARY VISITS BY YOUNG ADULTS. (10) ________________
11. Record YOUNG ADULT POPULATION OF LEGAL SERVICE AREA. (11) ________________
12. Divide (10) by (11) to get **Young Adult Library Visits per Young Adult.** (12) ________________

Form 8 Young Adult Library Visits Tally Sheet

Library/Entrance ______________________________ Date __________

Use one tally sheet each day per entrance. Enter number of hours during which data were collected. Count all young adults who enter the library for any reason.

A. Morning Visits. Morning is from _____ A.M. to noon, or _____ hours.

Total morning visits _____

B. Early Afternoon Visits. Early afternoon is from noon to _____ P.M., or _____ hours.

Total early afternoon visits _____

C. After-School Visits. "After School" is from _____ to _____, or _____ hours.

Total after-school visits _____

D. Evening Visits. Evening is from _____ to _____ (closing time) or _____ hours.

Total evening visits _____

TOTAL VISITS THIS DAY _____

Form 9 Building Use by Young Adults Data Collection Form

___ of ___

Library ______________________________ Date ____________

At sampling time, go quickly through the library and count the number of young adults in each of the following spaces.

Spaces	Users										
	Time:	Time:	Time:	Time:	Time:	Time:	Time:	Time:	Time:	Time:	Time:
Total											

Form 10 Furniture/Equipment Use by Young Adults Data Collection Form

___ of ___

Location or Department ______________________________ Date ____________

At sampling time, go quickly through the library and count the number of young adults using each of the following.

(Use Rate is Number in Use by young adults divided by Number Available.)

Furniture/Equipment	Number Available	OBSERVATIONS											
		Time:		Time:		Time:		Time:		Time:		Time:	
		# in Use	Use Rate	# in Use	Use Rate	# in Use	Use Rate	# in Use	Use Rate	# in Use	Use Rate	# in Use	Use Rate

Form 11 Homework Center Visits Sampling Work Sheet

1. Total of all weekday morning visits made during the sample periods. (Form 12, Section A.) (1) ________________
2. Number of weekday morning hours in the sample periods (e.g., 3 hours Monday morning + 3 hours Wednesday morning = 6). (2) ________________
3. (1) divided by (2) = average number of weekday morning library visits per hour. (3) ________________
4. Number of weekday morning hours the library is open each week. (4) ________________
5. (4) × (3) = the estimated number of weekday morning visits per week. (5) ________________
6. Repeat steps 1–5 for (a) early afternoon, (b) after school, (c) evening, (d) Saturday, and (e) Sunday hours, and record the estimated number of (6a) weekday early afternoon, (6b) weekday after school, (6c) weekday evening, (6d) Saturday, and (6e) Sunday visits per week.
   (6a) ________________
   (6b) ________________
   (6c) ________________
   (6d) ________________
   (6e) ________________
7. (5) + (6a) + (6b) + (6c) + (6d) + (6e) = the estimated number of homework center visits each week. (7) ________________
8. Multiply (7) by 12 if this is a summer sample week. This is the estimated Summer Homework Center Visits count. If Summer Homework Center Visits count was taken earlier, record it in (8). (8) ________________
9. Multiply (7) by 40 if this is a school year sample week. This is the estimated School Year Homework Center Visits count. If School Year Homework Visits count was taken earlier, record it in (9). (9) ________________
10. Add (8) and (9) to get the estimated ANNUAL NUMBER OF HOMEWORK CENTER VISITS. (10) ________________
11. Record YOUNG ADULT POPULATION OF LEGAL SERVICE AREA. (11) ________________
12. Divide (10) by (11) to get **Homework Center Visits per Young Adult.** (12) ________________

Form 12 Homework Center Visits Tally Sheet

Date ______________

Use one tally sheet each day. Enter number of hours during which data were collected. Count all young adults who use the homework center for any reason.

A. Morning Visits. Morning is from _____ A.M. to noon, or _____ hours.

Total morning visits _____

B. Early Afternoon Visits. Early afternoon is from noon to _____ P.M., or _____ hours.

Total early afternoon visits _____

C. After-School Visits. "After School" is from _____ to _____, or _____ hours.

Total after-school visits _____

D. Evening Visits. Evening is from _____ to _____ (closing time), or _____ hours.

Total evening visits _____

TOTAL VISITS THIS DAY _____

Form 13 In-Library Use of Young Adult Materials Log

Date ______________

Use one tally sheet each day. Enter times at the top of the form. At each time listed on the log, collect and count the young adult materials left for reshelving on tables, tops of shelves, floor, etc.

Type of Material	Time:	Time:	Time:	Time:	Time:	TOTAL
Paperbacks						
Hardcover Fiction						
Hardcover Nonfiction						
Magazines						
Cassette Tapes; CDs						
Other						
Other						
Other						
TOTAL						

Form 14 Young Adult In-Library Materials Use Tally Sheet

Please make a hash mark (/) each time you use one of these kinds of materials while you are in the library today. Place your completed form in one of the special boxes at the circulation desk or the exit when you leave the library. Thank you for your help!

Young adult books

Books from the adult or children's section

Young adult magazines

Other magazines

Reference books

Young adult cassette tapes or compact discs

Other cassette tapes or compact discs

Pamphlets

Something else?

How old are you? _____

Thanks again! Don't forget to leave your form in the box when you leave the library.

Form 14A Registro de Materiales Utilizados por Jovenes en la Biblioteca

Por favor indica con esta marca (/) cada vez que utilices alguno de los siguientes materiales, cuando estes en la biblioteca hoy. Devuelve el formulario completo en una de las cajas indicadas, las cuales estan ubicadas en la sección de circulación o en la salida de la biblioteca. ¡Gracias por tu ayuda!

Libros para jovenes

Libros de la sección de adultos o niños

Revistas juveniles

Otras revistas

Libros de referencia

Cassettes o discos compactos juveniles

Otros cassettes o discos compactos

Folletos

¿Algo más?

¿Cuántos años tienes? ____

¡Gracias de nuevo! No te olvides de dejar el formulario en la caja cuando salgas de la biblioteca.

Form 15 Young Adult Library Survey

Form #_____

1. How many items (books, magazines, tapes, etc.) did you check out today? _____

2. Were you looking for anything in particular in the library? YES NO
   If you were just browsing, skip down to question 3.

   If you were looking for particular things, please list them here:

   a. ______________________________

      Did you find it? YES NO

      Was it for school? YES NO

   b. ______________________________

      Did you find it? YES NO

      Was it for school? YES NO

   c. ______________________________

      Did you find it? YES NO

      Was it for school? YES NO

   (If you were looking for more than three things, please list them on the back.)

3. If you were just browsing and not looking for anything special, did you find anything interesting? YES NO

4. Did you come to the library for some completely different reason, such as attending a program or meeting a friend or using the restroom? YES NO

5. How old are you?_____

6. Is there anything else you want to tell us about the library? You may write on the back of the page if you want to.

Thank you for answering our questions today! Please leave this form in the marked box when you leave the library.

Form 15A Cuestionario para Jovenes Acerca de la Biblioteca

Formulario #_____

1. ¿Cuántos libros, revistas, cassettes y otros materiales prestaste hoy? _____

2. ¿Buscabas algo específico en la biblioteca? SÍ NO
   Si sólo estabas mirando pasa a la pregunta 3.

   Si buscabas algo específico, por favor escribe el titulo o autor aqui.

   a. ______________________________

   ¿Lo encontraste? SÍ NO

   ¿Era para la escuela? SÍ NO

   b. ______________________________

   ¿Lo encontraste? SÍ NO

   ¿Era para la escuela? SÍ NO

   c. ______________________________

   ¿Lo encontraste? SÍ NO

   ¿Era para la escuela? SÍ NO

   (Si buscabas más de tres cosas, por favor escríbelas atrás de la hoja.)

3. ¿Si sólo estabas mirando y no buscabas nada específico, encontraste algo interesante? SÍ NO

4. ¿Viniste a la biblioteca por alguna otra razón, como por ejemplo asistir a un programa, a encontrarte con un amigo o a utilizar los baños? SÍ NO

5. ¿Cuántos años tienes?_____

6. ¿Hay algo más que quisieras contarnos acerca de la biblioteca? Puedes hacerlo si quieres atrás de la hoja.

¡Gracias por contestar nuestras preguntas! Por favor deja este formulario en la caja indicada antes de salir de la biblioteca.

Form 16 Young Adult Library Survey Log

	(1) Title, subject, author				(2) Browsing		(3) Other	
	(a) Sought for school		*(b)* Not for school		*(a)* Browsers	*(b)* Found something	*(a)* Other	*(b)* Refused, blank, or missing
Form Number	*(c)* Found	*(d)* Not found	*(e)* Found	*(f)* Not found				
TOTAL								
	School items found	School items not found	Nonschool items found	Nonschool items not found	Number of browsers	Browsers finding something	Other	Not usable

Form 17 Young Adult Library Survey Summary

1. Number of questionnaires handed out (1) ________________
2. Questionnaires returned with usable title/subject/author or browsing answers (total of questions minus the total of columns 3a and 3b on Form 16) (2) ________________
3. Questionnaires with only "other" question checked (total of column 3a) (3) ________________
4. Usable questionnaires (subtotal of lines 2 and 3) (4) ________________
5. Questionnaires marked "refused," with no usable responses, or never returned (total of 3b) (5) ________________
6. Response rate (line 4 divided by line 1) (6) ________________

Young Adult Fill Rate

7. Title/subject/authors sought (total of columns 1c, d, e, and f) (7) ________________
8. Title/subject/authors found (total of columns 1c and 1e) (8) ________________
9. Title/subject/authors fill rate (line 8 divided by line 7) (9) ________________
10. Number of browsers (total of column 2a) (10) ________________
11. Number of browsers finding something (total of column 2b) (11) ________________
12. Browsing fill rate (line 11 divided by line 10) (12) ________________
13. **Young Adult Fill Rate**

    (13a) total of line 8 and line 11 (13a) ________________

    (13b) total of line 7 and line 10 (13b) ________________

    (13c) 13a divided by 13b (13c) ________________

Homework Fill Rate

14. Title/subject/authors sought for school (total of column 1c and 1d) (14) ________________
15. Title/subject/authors sought for school and found (total of column 1c) (15) ________________
16. **Homework Fill Rate** (line 15 divided by line 14) (16) ________________

Form 18 Young Adult Information Transaction Tally Sheet

Form # ______________________ Date ______________________

Library ______________________ Time period ______________________

1. For each young adult information transaction, put one hash mark (/) in section A, B, C, or D. Make one hash mark per transaction.
2. Count questions by users who are 12 to 18 *or* by adults such as parents or teachers who are asking questions on behalf of young people.
3. An information transaction is a contact that involves the knowledge, use, recommendations, interpretation, or instruction in the use of one or more information sources by a member of the library staff. Include information and referral transactions and requests by phone, mail, or fax as well as in person. Count readers' advisory requests.
4. For users with multiple questions, record each question as a separate transaction if it deals with a new concern.

A. Information Transactions Completed Today (user has received the requested information on the same day)

Total A _____

B. Information Transactions Redirected (e.g., to another department, library, or a nonlibrary source)

Total B _____

C. Information Transactions Not Completed Today (includes those completed at another time)

Total C _____

D. Other Questions (includes directional questions and other questions not included in the definition of reference transaction above)

Total D _____

Form 19 Children, Young Adult, and Adult Information Transaction Tally Sheet

Form # ______________________ Date ______________________

Library ______________________ Time period ______________________

A. Information Transactions Completed Today (user has received the requested information on the same day)

Children (0–11)	Young adult (12–18)	Adult (over 18)
Total A	Total A	Total A

B. Information Transactions Redirected (e.g., to another department, library, or a nonlibrary source)

Children (0–11)	Young adult (12–18)	Adult (over 18)
Total B	Total B	Total B

C. Information Transactions Not Completed Today (includes those completed at another time)

Children (0–11)	Young adult (12–18)	Adult (over 18)
Total C	Total C	Total C

D. Other Questions (includes directional questions and other questions not included in the definition of reference transaction on Form 18)

Children (0–11)	Young adult (12–18)	Adult (over 18)
Total D	Total D	Total D

Form 20 Young Adult Program Attendance Log

Library ______________________

Month ______________________

Date	Name of Program	Number Attending
	TOTAL	

Form 21 Program Attendance by Young Adults Log

Library ____________________

Month ____________________

Date	Name of Program	Total Attending	YAs Attending
	TOTAL		

Form 22 Young Adult School Contact Log

Library ______________________

Month ______________________

Date	School	Type of Contact

Total Number of School Contacts ______________________

Form 23 Young Adult Community Contact Log

Library ____________________

Month ____________________

Date	Community Contact (name of organization, person, etc.)	Phone	Address

Total Number of Community Contacts ____________________

Form 24 Individual Youth Participant Record

Name ______________________________

Address ______________________________

____

Telephone ______________________________

Birth Date __________ School ______________

Library Participation Activities

Date	Activity	Total Hours

Form 25 Youth Participation Tally Sheet

Name	Activities	Total Hours

Index

Virginia A. Walter is currently assistant professor in the department of Library and Information Science at the University of California at Los Angeles. She has an MLS degree from the University of California at Berkeley and a Ph.D. in Public Administration from the University of Southern California. She teaches courses in library management and library services for children. Her research and writing deal primarily with the evaluation of public library services, the use of volunteers in public libraries, and children's information needs and information resources. She is the author of *Output Measures for Public Library Service to Children: A Manual of Standardized Procedures* (Chicago: American Library Association, 1992) and *War and Peace Literature for Children and Young Adults: A Resource Guide to Significant Issues* (Phoenix, Ariz.: Oryx, 1993).

Before joining the faculty at UCLA, Walter worked for more than twenty years in public libraries in California. She has been a Children's Librarian, Young Adult Librarian, Branch Library Manager, Regional Library Administrator, and Central Library Department Head. Most recently, she was the Children's Services Coordinator at Los Angeles Public Library.